国际导游与领队

王　宁　彭厚坤　编著

WUHAN UNIVERSITY PRESS
武汉大学出版社

图书在版编目(CIP)数据

国际导游与领队:英文/王宁,彭厚坤编著.—武汉:武汉大学出版社,2018.1

ISBN 978-7-307-19781-7

Ⅰ.国… Ⅱ.①王… ②彭… Ⅲ.导游—业务—英文
Ⅳ.F590.633

中国版本图书馆 CIP 数据核字(2017)第 284611 号

责任编辑:刘小娟　　责任校对:周卫思　　装帧设计:张希玉

出版发行:**武汉大学出版社**　(430072　武昌　珞珈山)
(电子邮件:whu_publish@163.com　网址:www.stmpress.cn)
印刷:广东虎彩云印刷有限公司
开本:720×1000　1/16　印张:11.75　字数:229 千字
版次:2018 年 1 月第 1 版　2018 年 1 月第 1 次印刷
ISBN 978-7-307-19781-7　定价:39.00 元

前　言

随着中国旅游业的深入发展，旅游业将成为中国国民经济战略性支柱产业。近年来，中国的出入境旅游发展迅猛，中国已经成为世界第三大旅游目的地。2014年，中国的出境旅游人数已经突破1亿，成为全球第一大旅游客源国。未来五到十年，中国的出境旅游人数将达到5亿。为了适应中国出入境旅游发展和旅游管理专业高等教育发展的需要，我们编写了本书，供各大专院校旅游管理专业学生使用，亦可供涉外导游、出境领队和出入境旅游运营等从业人员阅读和参考。

本书是根据编者多年积累的教学实践和丰富的旅游行业工作经验，针对旅游管理专业高等教育的特点和旅游行业特征，并参考了国内外的相关出版物编写而成的。本书尤其强调实用性和操作性，注重涉外导游与出境领队工作的程序、环节、要点，突出涉外导游与出境领队业务的应用、操作方面的内容，力求使读者能学以致用，以解决工作中的实际问题。全书共分为三个部分19个单元，每个单元又由课文、口语技能、练习作业、课内练习、扩展阅读等5个部分构成。第一部分"导游"，共8个单元，主要介绍接团、入住、用餐、观光游览、现场导游、旅游购物到最后送团整个导游服务业务过程，涉及接待、行李处理、欢迎词、导游词、欢送词、现场讲解、景点翻译、菜名翻译、购物服务等环节的流程和语言技能训练。第二部分"出境领队"，共5个单元，主要介绍国际航班乘坐、出入境手续办理、购物退税申请、紧急特殊情况处理和自由活动翻译服务等主要出境领队业务过程和语言技能训练。第三部分"实用旅游英文写作"，共6个单元，主要介绍出入境旅游业务应用文的认读与拟写，包括旅游咨询、预订与确认、旅行通知（出游通知、催款、旅行警示）、旅行社业务往来信函、游程与旅游合同、投诉处理等，通过范文帮助读者熟悉和掌握各种文体的写作格式、内容要点和常用句型与语言特点，并能熟练地运用这些实用文体。

本书的编写得到了业界专家和院校学者的大力支持。重庆假日国际旅行社有限公司副总经理、高级翻译杨顺华先生审读了本书,并提出了许多宝贵的意见,在此一并致谢。

由于编者水平有限,书中难免有不足之处,敬请读者指正。

编　者

2017 年 10 月

Contents

Part Ⅰ
Tour Guiding
导游

Unit 1 Meeting the Group at the Airport
机场接团

【内容导读】

本单元介绍机场接团的程序、注意事项，以及欢迎词的内容及格式。

【学习目标】

通过本单元学习，要熟练掌握机场接团的程序以及欢迎词的内容、格式、常用语和句型。

【学习要点】

欢迎词的撰写。

Text

As a tour guide, you are the representative of a travel service and you are often the only one that the tour group members will meet. The way in which the tour guide carries out his / her duties has great impacts on the functioning of the tour. The impression the tour group members will have of both of the travel service and China will be based on the professionalism of the tour guide.

The tour guide should be fluent in oral proficiency and be knowledgeable about the city and the country in which he/she is working. In addition to operating the tour, the tour guide should be able to be a "resource person"①, willing to answer questions and ready to be helpful during a trip. The tour guide must constantly check the group, airplane tickets, and everything he/she is responsible.

Oral Skills

Ⅰ. Meeting the Group at the Airport

Procedure and Useful Patterns

Step 1 Preparation.

Before you go to the airport to meet the group you must get everything ready for the group.

1. Check with the airport on arrival time, and arrive at the airport before the flight arrives.

2. Get a sign (a signboard or a piece of paper) with the logo of your travel service, the group number or the name of the tour leader of this group on it, so that they can easily find out their local guide when they are coming out of the airport.

3. Get everything ready for the group including the itinerary, hotel room reservation, hotel rooming list, hotel room key cards if possible.

Step 2 Recognizing the tour leader and greeting the group.

As a local guide, you just hold up the sign and stand in an obvious place in the airport lobby waiting for the coming out of the group. For recognizing the tour leader and greeting the group, you may use the following useful patterns:

Are you Miss/Mr. . . . ?

D1119 group?

Welcome to . . . . I'm . . . your local guide from. . . . Nice to meet you.

Then you need to show the guests to the tour coach waiting outside of the airport. You may use:

If you would like to move this way?

Follow me, please. / This way, please. Our bus is waiting outside.

Step 3 Dealing with the luggage.

Before you get on the bus, you need to tell the guests how to deal with their luggage, where to put the luggage, and who will take care of the luggage. You need also count the luggage pieces and handover the luggage with the luggage boy before you leave for the hotel. You may use the following useful patterns:

Please leave your checked luggage here.

We have a luggage boy to take care of them.

Don't worry about that. They will be sent to the hotel.

Just take your carry-on with you. And let's get on the bus.

Step 4 Getting on the tour coach (on the bus).

When getting on the tour coach, before you leave, the first thing you will do is that you must make sure that everyone is here on the bus. Then, greet the group again and tell them where to go.

You may use the following useful patterns:

Is everyone here?

Anyone missing?

OK, here we go.

Now we're heading for the hotel. It's about ... minutes' ride.

Sample Dialogue

(Mr. Zhao = the local guide; Mr. Green = the tour leader of the group)

Mr. Zhao is at the airport to meet a tour group from U.S.

Mr. Zhao: Excuse me. Are you Mr. Green from U.S.?

Mr. Green: Yes.

Mr. Zhao: Nice to meet you, Mr. Green. Welcome to Chengdu. My name is Zhao Xing and I am your local guide in Chengdu.

Mr. Green: Nice to meet you, Zhao. How are you?

Mr. Zhao: Fine, thank you. How was your trip?

Mr. Green: It was good. We had a very pleasant trip.

Mr. Zhao: Great! Is everybody here now?

Mr. Green: Well, let me see. Yes, everyone is here.

Mr. Zhao: Good. (Turn to the group members) Hello, everybody. Our bus is waiting outside. Are you ready to leave?

Mr. Green: Yes. We are ready.

Mr. Zhao: OK, please follow me to the bus. This way, please. (A moment later) Everyone, your attention, please. Please leave your checked luggage here and just take your carry-on with you. We have a luggage boy to take care of your luggage.

Don't worry about that. Your luggage will be sent directly to your hotel room.

Mr. Green: Great!

Mr. Zhao: If you are ready, let's get on the bus.

Ⅱ. Making a Welcome Speech

A welcome speech marks the start of a tour. The focus of the speech is always the tourists and the goal is to make them look forward to whatever is coming next.

In your speech, the following items should be included:

1. Extending a warm welcome to the group.

You may say:

Good morning, everyone. Welcome to....

Please allow me to say "welcome to you" on behalf of... Travel Service.

2. Making an introduction to your team and make sure you'll be always at their service.

As a tour guide, you must remember that you are doing a team work. The team is made up of the guide, the driver, and even the luggage boy. When you are introducing your team to the group, it is better to put the driver in the first place, and the guide (yourself) the second.

Useful patterns:

Please allow me to introduce my team to you.

May I introduce my team to you?

This is our driver Mr.....

Both of us are very glad to be of your service.

We'll be with you. And we'll try our best to help you and make your stay in... a very pleasant one.

3. Giving a brief account of tour arrangements.

Tell the group what they'll do, where to go, when to go.

Useful patterns:

I'm talking about the schedule for....

Tomorrow morning we'll go to... to do....

The day after tomorrow, we'll pay a visit to....

4. Making a brief introduction to the local city.

(1) General information (including: name, location, territory, population, history).

(2) Outstanding features of the local city.

Useful patterns:

be located in/be situated in / lies or stand in.

cover an area of... square kilometers.

with a total population of....

5. Giving best wishes to them.

Useful patterns:

Wish you have a pleasant stay in. . . .

Hope you have a wonderful tour.

Hope you will enjoy your visit.

Sample Welcome Speech 1

Good morning, ladies and gentlemen.

Welcome to Chongqing!

Please allow me to introduce my team to you. Well, this is our driver Mr. Hu. He is a very experienced driver. He has 20 years of driving under his belt. So you are in safe hands. I'm Frederick, your local guide here in Chongqing.

Both of us are from... International Travel Service, and we are very glad to be of your service. During your stay in Chongqing, we'll be with you. And we'll try our best to help you and make your stay in Chongqing a very pleasant one. So if you have any questions, any requests, or if you need our help, just let me know. Or, when you go back to U. S . you may regretfully say "Oh! I should have let Frederick know this or that", it will be too late. OK, just feel free to come to Frederick. And we highly appreciate your understanding and your co-operation.

Now, I'm talking about the itinerary. We'll stay in Chongqing for two days.

For the first day (tomorrow) we'll have a whole day city tour. We'll first go to the zoo to see the lovely panda bears. Then, we'll move to the ancient town of Ciqikou. After that we'll pay a visit to the China Three Gorges Museum and the People's Great Hall of Chongqing which is known as the landmark and the symbol of Chongqing. After dinner we'll go to enjoy the charming night view of the Mountain City[②].

And for the second day (the day after tomorrow) we'll have a day tour driving to Dazu Rock Carvings, a world cultural heritage site in Chongqing[③]. In the evening we'll get on board the cruse and leave Chongqing to tour the famous Yangtze River Gorges.

Well, to help you have a better understanding of our city, I'd like to give you a brief introduction to Chongqing. Chongqing is located in the southwestern part of China, where the two rivers (the Yangtze and the Jialing) come together. The two rivers divide the city of Chongqing into three parts, making the central part of the city peninsula—shaped. Chongqing is one of the four municipalities directly under the central government in China. It covers an area of 82,000 square kilometers (including the rural area), with a total population of over 30 million people, and over 6 million in the city proper. It is also the largest city in the west part of China. Chongqing is both an ancient and young city. It is ancient because it has a history of over 3,000 years. It was the capital of the ancient Ba Kingdom, and it was once the war capital of China during the World War Two. It has been keeping the name Chongqing for 800 years. Do you know the meaning of the name of our city Chongqing? Oh, yes. You know, in Chinese language, "Chong" means "double", and "Qing" means "celebration". Chongqing is a city of double celebrations. Some people say that Chongqing is a city of good luck. I hope everyone in this group will have your double celebrations here in Chongqing. Chongqing is a young city in terms of municipality.④ It has become the fourth municipality in China (directly under the central government) since 1997.

So what's special about Chongqing you may ask? Well, to best describe the city of Chongqing, I got three h-words. The first h-word about Chongqing is "hilly". As you can see, there are rolling and rising hills around Chongqing. And the whole city is on hills. I mean, all the buildings in the city are scattered over the mountain slopes, layer upon layer. Hence it is known as the "Mountain City" in China. Because of the mountains and hills, the roads and streets in this city are narrow and steep. And you can seldom see people ride a bike in Chongqing, because it is very difficult for people to do that. "If you ride a bike in Chongqing", someone said, "it's not you ride a bike, but the bike rides you". I remember that in 1980s an American journalist paid a visit to Chongqing, after he came back to U. S., he wrote an article to introduce Chongqing, it is titled "The only city in China without a bicycle". Yes, it is true. Chongqing is the only city in China without a bicycle.

Another h-word about Chongqing is "hot". I mean the hot climate. It is very hot in Chongqing, especially in summer time. Sometimes in summer in Chongqing the temperature is as high as 42 or 43 degrees centigrade (107 or 109 degrees Fahrenheit). Even in winter it is not cold, the temperature never goes below zero, and it seldom snows. It is warm. So, Chongqing is known as one of the three "Heating Ovens" in China.

Not only the climate is hot, but also the food in Chongqing is hot. Have you ever heard of the hot-pot in Chongqing? Have you tried? Hot-pot is a very typical local flavor popular among the local people. We have hot-pot for gathering, big celebration, even for family reunion. We just put a pot on the table, and get almost everything hot and spicy into the pot, like chili sauce, peppers, gingers, garlic, or whatever, and any food, and then we sit around the table eating while cooking. It tastes hot and very delicious. If you would like to have a try, just let me know.

Well, the girls in Chongqing are hot as well. Most of the young girls in Chongqing have a very strong character. Yes, they are warm-hearted and very active. They behave quickly and act boldly in working, speaking and dressing. They are known as spicy Chongqing girls.

"Humid" is the third h-word about Chongqing. I'm sure you have sensed that. The air here is always wet, especially in summer time. You'll feel your skin is always sticky. This is because the whole city is surrounded by rolling and rising hills, it is typical of basin landform, and there are two big rivers flowing through the city, it steams a lot every day. In winter, there is always heavy fog in Chongqing. Even in summer, most of the time the whole city is shrouded in light mists. So the city of Chongqing is also known as the "City of Fog" in China.

It is my sincere hope that you will enjoy your visit to Chongqing. Thank you.

Sample Welcome Speech 2

Good evening, ladies and gentlemen.

I am delighted that you have chosen to spend your holiday in Paris and I hope that your visit to our city will be a memorable experience.

Paris is a majestic city. It is a city of culture, romance, gastronomy, design and fashion. It is also a city on the move, a city of daring. With the opening of new museum, world-class sporting events, festive and popular urban happenings, Paris is a capital that never sleeps. ⑤

Whether you are a new comer or already familiar with the Paris scene, there is a vast choice awaiting you: over 1,800 classified monuments, 170 museums, 145 theaters and 380 cinemas. Some of the cultural sites of the capital are absolute "musts" and among the most visited monuments in the world. Several of them have UNESCO⑥ world heritage status.

Paris, however, is not just a historic city. Its riverbanks and neighborhoods, some of which retain a village atmosphere, are an invitation to stroll and sightseeing. ⑦

Paris, the eternal, City of Lights, original, modern, and creative is all yours. Whether you are already "in love" with our city or here for the first time, please make yourself at home.

Welcome to Paris!

Notes

① the tour guide should be able to be a "resource person" 导游应该是一位"专家"

② Mountain City 山城

③ Dazu Rock Carvings, a world cultural heritage site in Chongqing 大足石刻,重庆的世界文化遗产

④ Chongqing is a young city in terms of municipality. 就直辖市而言,重庆是一座年轻的城市。

⑤ With the opening of new museum, world-class sporting events, festive and popular urban happenings, Paris is a capital that never sleeps. 新开张的博物馆、世界级的体育赛事、节庆般的且受人喜爱的市区活动,使巴黎成为一座不夜城。

⑥ UNESCO (United Nations Educational, Scientific, and Cultural Organization) 联合国教科文组织

⑦ Its riverbanks and neighborhoods, some of which retain a village atmosphere, are an invitation to stroll and sightseeing. 它的河岸和街区,有些保留着乡村的氛围,是漫步和观光的好去处。

Words and Expressions

professionalism	*n.* 职业精神;职业水准或特性;职业化
handover	*v.* 移交;交接
cruse	*n.* 游轮
landmark	*n.* 地标;里程碑
municipality	*n.* 市;直辖市
peninsula-shaped	*adj.* 半岛状的
hilly	*adj.* 多山的;多丘陵的
Fahrenheit	*n.* 华氏温度
boldly	*adv.* 大胆地
spicy	*adj.* 辛辣的
shroud	*v.* 笼罩;覆盖

majestic	*adj.* 雄伟的;壮丽的
gastronomy	*n.* 美食
eternal	*adj.* 永恒的;永久的

luggage boy	行李员
carry-on	手提行李;随身携带的行李
tour leader	领队
panda bears	(口语)大熊猫
be of one's service	为某人服务;为某人效劳
war capital	战时首都;陪都
Heating Ovens	火炉
basin landform	盆地地貌
hot-pot	火锅
be shrouded in...	笼罩在…之中
on the move	在移动中;处于动感状态

Assignments

1. Write a brief introduction for your hometown.

The following points should be included:

(1) General information about your hometown, including the name, location, population and history.

(2) Outstanding features of your hometown.

(3) In 300-500 words.

2. Translate the following into English.

(1) 我代表中国旅行社对各位的到来表示热烈的欢迎。

(2) 我们非常高兴为你们提供服务。

(3) 这座小城位于涪江与嘉陵江的交汇处,三面环水,景色秀丽。

(4) 重庆多山,以山城著称。

(5) 这座山常年笼罩在云雾之中。

In-class Practice

Role-play

Divide the class into groups to role-play according to the following situations.

Situation 1

A local guide called Li Ming is waiting for a tour group from Canada at the airport. The tour leader of this group is named Kollins. Now the passengers are coming out with their luggage. Li Ming has not met Kollins before, so he is about to

- locate the tour leader and the group;
- introduce himself;
- welcome the group;
- show them onto the bus and help deal with their luggage.

Situation 2

A group of tourists are visiting your hometown. As a local guide, you are to

- make a welcome speech to the group;
- introduce them something unique about your hometown.

Broaden Your Mind

China's Family Planning

Excessive population growth is an extremely serious problem facing the contemporary world. Each minute, the earth's population is increased by 160 people. In face of this problem, the UN Population Fund sounded a warning to the international community: Lacking prompt and determined moves to control population and maintain a balance between consumption and development, the world population would be 12.5 billion people by the middle of the next century and humanity be unable to develop further.

The global emergence of the population question poses a serious challenge to many countries and regions. For a populous developing country like China the challenge posed by the population question not only has a bearing on the survival and development of the Chinese nation but also affects the stability and prosperity of all human society.

Over the vast territory of China, the space suited for people to live and engage in economic activities is limited and population distribution is extremely uneven. A large part of its land is mountain, plateau, desert, hilly and basin area that is unsuited for living. Cultivated area in China accounts for only one-tenth of its territory. "Food is the first necessity of the people." To solve the problem of feeding the largest population in the world is a big challenge to China.

China's abundant labour force is of course conducive to development. Now, nearly 20 million young people reach working age in China every year, and most of them need jobs. Although the state has adopted various measures to open up channels for employment and satisfactory results have been achieved, there are still considerably large amounts of people who are in job-waiting or recessive unemployment.

It is a natural choice that the Chinese government has made to implement family planning, control population growth and improve the life quality of the population a basic state policy on the basis of a wish to make the state strong and powerful, the nation prosperous and the people happy.

From the early 1970s, the Chinese government had become increasingly deeply aware that the over-rapid growth of population was unfavourable to economic and social development and decided to energetically carry out one-child policy?（that each couple is urged to have no more than one child）in both urban and rural areas and integrated the plan for population development into the plan of national economic and social development.

Family planning in China had its benefits, and its drawbacks. For example, it helped reduce the population by about 30 million people in its first 20 years. A drawback is that there are now millions of siblings-less people(数以百万计的人没有兄弟姐妹), and in China siblings are very important. Once the parent generation gets older, the children help take care of them, and the work is usually equally split among the siblings. Another benefit of the implementation of the one-child law is that it reduced the fertility rate（生育率）from about 5.4 children born per woman, to about 1.8 children born per woman in the 1970s.

Unit 2 Group Check in
团队入住

【内容导读】

本单元介绍旅游团队在酒店办理入住手续的程序，以及导游在办理团队入住时的操作流程、注意事项及常用英语句型等内容。

【学习目标】

掌握团队入住的操作流程、注意事项及常用英语句型。

【学习要点】

办理团队入住的程序。

Text

Check in with a Hotel

After a tiring journey, the guests are often confused, jet-lagged, suffering from a sudden change in environment, climate etc. The guests are only concerned with being registered as quickly and efficiently as possible and then shown to their rooms. So, the hotel room reservations should be made well before the arrival of the visitors.

To help a tour group check-in at a hotel, the first thing you will do is to collect the guests' passports for group registration. The receptionist will help to fill out the registration forms with the guests' name, nationality, address, passport number, and etc. When everything is in order, the receptionist will distribute to the guests the key cards of the rooms. It is a good idea that the key cards be handed to the tour leader who is supposed to understand the preferences of the group members much better than you do①, and thus he can make each one more satisfied with the room distribution②.

Another favor you can do for the group is to get some cards with the hotel name, address and telephone number and distribute them among the guests. It is of help for them to find the way back to the hotel if they go out themselves in their free time.

Oral Skills

Procedure and Useful Patterns

Step 1 Introducing hotel facilities.

1. General information (name, location, and surroundings of the hotel).

You may use the following useful patterns:

Well, I have reserved rooms for you. The hotel we' ll stay in is Hilton Hotel. It is a five-star hotel and one of the best we can find for you here in Chongqing. The hotel is located right in the downtown area. There is a supermarket, grocery stores and restaurants around the hotel. So it is convenient for you.

2. Hotel facilities (meals, business center, and entertainments in the hotel).

You may use the following useful patterns:

There is a western-styled buffet and a Chinese restaurant on the second floor in the hotel. For breakfast (breakfast is included), you just go to the buffet from 7:00 a. m. to 10:00 a. m. by showing your key card. If you want to try Chinese food for your dinner, you can go to the Chinese restaurant in the hotel.

For fax, E-mail, or photocopy, just go to the business center on the fourth floor in the hotel.

There is a swimming pool on the ninth floor of the hotel. If you want to go swimming, just go there by showing your key card.

Step 2 Collecting passports.

You may use the following useful patterns:

Later on when we arrive at the hotel we' ll have a group check in. I need your passports for the group check in. Please have your passports ready. After the group check in I' ll give back your passports.

Step 3 Distributing key cards.

You may use the following useful patterns:

I' ve got the key cards from the hotel. Now I' m distributing the key cards to you.

OK, this is for... (sb.). / this is a single room for... (sb.). / Room 1216 for... (sb.).

Step 4 Showing guests to rooms.

You may use the following useful patterns:

Well, have you all got your key cards? OK, you just go up directly to your room. The elevator is over there. This way please.

See you later.

Step 5 Having a check with the guests' rooms.

After the group check in is finished, you get back the guests' passports from the hotel front office. You'd better go up to the guests' rooms to give back their passports and have a check with their rooms to make sure that there are not any problems with their rooms.

You may use the following useful patterns:

How is your room?

Is your room OK?

I'm glad you like your room.

I'm pleased that you enjoyed your room.

Sample Dialogue

(Mr. Zhao = the local guide; Mr. Green = the tour leader of the group)

The tour group has arrived at the hotel.

Mr. Zhao: OK, everybody. Here we are. This is the Hilton Hotel we'll stay in.

Guest A: Oh, it's a nice hotel.

Mr. Zhao: Now, I need your passports for the group check in. (Turn to the tour leader) Mr. Green, if you would like to collect their passports for me?

Mr. Green: Sure. (Turn to the group) Everybody, please give me your passports.

Guests: Here you are.

Mr. Green: Mr. Zhao, here are the passports of our group. It's 24.

Mr. Zhao: Thank you. I'll go to the front desk for our group check-in. Just stay in the lobby and have a short rest.

Mr. Green: OK.

Mr. Zhao: Mr. Green, I've got the key cards from the hotel. Would you please distribute them among the guests?

Mr. Green: Of course. (Turn to the group) Now I'm distributing the key cards to you. OK, this is for Mr. Bake. Room 1216 for Brown. . . .

Mr. Zhao: Well, have you all got your key cards?

Guests: Yes, we got it.

Mr. Zhao: Now, you just go up directly to your room. The elevator is over there. This way please.

Guest B: Thank you, Mr. Zhao. By the way, could you tell us when and where to have our breakfast?

Mr. Zhao: Well, you just go to the buffet on the second floor in the hotel for breakfast from 7:00 a. m. to 10:00 a. m. by showing your key card.

Guest B: Thank you.

Mr. Zhao: You are welcome.

Notes

① It is a good idea that the key cards be handed to the tour leader who is supposed to understand the preferences of the group members much better than you do. . . . 最好将钥匙牌交由领队分发,领队比你更了解团队成员的喜好……

② room distribution 客房分配

Words and Expressions

confused	*adj.* 困惑的;糊涂的
jet-lagged	*adj.* 有时差反应的
grocery	*n.* 食品杂货店
buffet	*n.* 自助餐厅
photocopy	*n.* & *v.* 复印
distribute	*vt.* 分配
elevator	*n.* 电梯
check in	登记入住;办理入住手续
be concerned with	关注…;关心…
key card	钥匙牌
have a check with	检查;核实,核对

Assignments

Translate the following into English:

(1) 我们要入住的酒店是一家五星级豪华酒店。

(2) 我需要大家的护照办理团队入住手续,请大家准备好护照。

(3) 这家酒店坐落在长江边上,景色漂亮,环境宁静。

(4) 请大家早上 7 点至 9 点到酒店二楼的自助餐厅用早餐。

(5) 进入房间后请检查一下房间,以确保没有问题。

In-class Practice

Role-play

Your group has just checked in with the hotel. Work in pairs and make a dialogue according to the following situations:

Situation 1

A guest wants to change to a room on the non-smoking floor.

Situation 2

A guest wants to know when, where, and how to have breakfast in the hotel.

Broaden Your Mind

Traditional Chinese Festivals

Spring Festival

The Chinese Spring Festival or the Chinese Lunar New Year is the most important and widely observed festival throughout the whole country. The dates for this annual celebration are determined by the lunar calendar rather than the Gregorian calendar, so the timing of the holiday varies from late January to early February.

To the Chinese, the Spring Festival is a time for family union, for visiting relatives and friends, for good wishes for the coming year. Before the eve of the New Year, everyone tries to come back home from every corner of the country to join the entire family, just like Americans' practice for Christmas, to greet the New Year.

A New Year big dinner is served. After the meal, the table is cleared, dishes washed and put away. Then it is time to undertake final preparations to meet the New Year.

At midnight following a nice family banquet on the New Year' s Eve, the young members of the family would bow and pay their respects to the parents and elders.

In the morning, people put on their new clothes and shoes. Men, with their wives, call on relatives and friends to wish them a "Happy and Prosperous New Year". The caller is served tea with sweet-meats; melon seeds, both red and black; and fruits and delicacies. Before leaving, the well-wisher present gifts of money wrapped in red paper to all the unmarried children of the family.

Starting from the New Year' s Day, people began going out to visit friends and relatives, taking with them gifts such as fruits, wines, flowers, etc. The entire fortnight was a time for socializing and amusement. Common expressions heard at this time are: "Guonian Hao" (Happy New Year), and "Bainian" (to congratulate the New Year).

The burning of long strings of firecrackers accompanies the Eve of the New Year. Most adults and children do not touch their bed the whole night, busy at all kinds of activities welcoming the New Year.

Dragon Boat Festival

The Dragon Boat Festival, also called the Duanwu Festival, is celebrated on the fifth day of the fifth month according to the Chinese calendar. For thousands of years, the festival has been marked by eating Zongzi (glutinous rice wrapped to form a pyramid using bamboo or reed leaves) and racing dragon boats.

The festival is best known for its dragon-boat races. This regatta (赛舟会) commemorates the death of Qu Yuan , an honest minister of the State of Chu during the Warring States Period (475 B. C. -221 B. C.). Qu Yuan was upright, loyal and highly esteemed for his wise counsel that brought peace and prosperity to the state. However, when a dishonest and corrupt prince vilified Qu, he was disgraced and dismissed from office. Realizing that the country was now in the hands of evil and corrupt officials, Qu committed suicide by drowning himself in the Miluo River on the fifth day of the fifth month.

During the Duanwu Festival, a glutinous rice pudding called Zongzi is eaten to symbolize the rice offerings to Qu. Ingredients such as beans, lotus seeds (莲子), chestnuts(栗子), pork fat and the golden yolk of a salted duck egg are often added to the glutinous rice. The pudding is then wrapped with bamboo leaves which give a special flavor to the food.

Mid-autumn Festival

The Mid-autumn Festival also called Moon Festival, falls on the 15th day of the 8th lunar month because the 8th lunar month is mid-autumn and the 15th is the middle of that month. On that night the moon is supposed to be brighter and fuller than any other night. In China, a full moon is symbolic of family reunion, which is why that day is also known as the "Day of Reunion".

In ancient China, the moon was considered by scholars as a symbol of brightness, purity, and goodness. Poets of the past wrote many beautiful odes to the moon. Not only was the moon an inspiration to writers but it was also a source of many myths and legends. The most popular myth was a story about a woman named Chang'e who flew to the moon and lived in the Moon Palace.

During this festival, people eat the moon cake, which is made of wheat flour and sweet stuffing such as sugar and lotus seed powder. The festival is a time for families to gather to burn incense and eat fruits in addition to the moon cake. The cake is traditionally cut into pieces that equal the number of people in the family. While tradition abounds during this festival, the essence of this festival is the harmony and happiness of family life, which is something that can be understood by all.

Unit 3 A Guide Speech
导游词

【内容导读】

本单元通过导游词实例范文，介绍英文导游词的撰写方法，包括导游词的格式、结构、内容和景点介绍的方法。

【学习目标】

掌握英文导游词的撰写方法。

【学习要点】

英文导游词中关于景点的介绍方法。

Text

Making a Good Guide Speech

A guide speech is a speech made by the tour guide to give a narration or introduction to the landscape visited by the group. A guide speech conveys information about a place, or a historical period, or a personage, or an event, or a part of a particular culture. Usually, it is made by the tour guide when leading the group on a site tour, or on a coach tour. By this way, the guide communicates with the tourists and transmits cultural knowledge to them.

When you are giving or writing a guide speech, the following points should be included in your speech.

1. Opening statement.

The opening statement is an introduction to draw the attention of the tourists, to outline the theme of the tour, and to provide direction or an idea of what is coming up. It includes greetings, precautions, schedule and arrangements. The tour guide should tell the guests where to go (destination), what to see and what to do (activity), how long will it take to get there? And how long will you stay at the site?

2. Introduction to the landscape.

A. General information about the landscape.

It is a brief introduction to the spot, including the name, location, range and area, history, and nature of the spot, helping the guests have a general understanding of the landscape.

B. Detailed introduction.

It is a detailed explanation about the spot, like the genesis (cause), cultural background, main contents, etc., but you need to focus on the key points and the outstanding features of the landscape, helping them have a comprehensive understanding of the landscape.

Oral Skills

Sample Speech 1

A Visit to the Zoo

Is everyone here? OK, here we go.

Good morning, everyone. Now we are heading for the zoo to see the panda bears. It's about 30 minutes' ride from the hotel. And we'll stay there for about one hour and a half. Then we'll move to another spot. So now I'd like to introduce you something about the zoo and the giant pandas.

The zoo is located in the western suburbs of our city. It was built in 1953. Embraced by rolling and rising hills, the zoo is U-shaped and covers an area of 400,000 square meters. It's really a big one. Consisting of over 20 feeding areas and exhibition halls, it boasts more than 150 species of wild animals, among which the most precious are giant pandas, the lesser (red) pandas, the south China tigers, and the golden monkeys. Well, today we'll just walk around the lower part of the zoo to see pandas, tigers and monkeys. We won't go up hills to see the other animals. This is because if we do so, it will be a whole day. Then our babies will suffer from hunger and tiredness.

You know, pandas inhabit only in China's Sichuan and Gansu Provinces. They have a history of millions of years. They were of the same age as the dinosaurs. As we all know, all the dinosaurs have become extinct, while the giant pandas survived. ① But now the giant pandas are also in danger of extinction. And the total number of giant pandas in the world is less than 1,000. There are some possible reasons for that.

The first reason is the change of the climate and environment. Especially, in recent years, large areas of forests have been destroyed by our mankind, the temperature on earth is getting higher and higher, and the habitat of pandas is becoming smaller and smaller.

The second reason might be their poor multiply capability[②]. You know, the giant pandas like living alone. They don't like living in groups. It is very hard for a female panda to be in a family way. Normally, a panda can live only 20 to 25 years. But a female panda can give birth to baby panda only once or twice during her life. And when the baby panda was born, it was very small in size. Do you know the weight of a newly-born baby panda? Just guess.

"20 *ounces, I guess.*"

"*Maybe*, 5 *kilos*?"

No, not that much. Actually, it's only 100 to 150 grams, very tiny, like a newly-born baby mouse. And it's really a hard work for mother panda to take care of her baby and let the baby grow up healthily. So our biologists are trying their effort to help them with artificial insemination. Through years of hard work, we have made some progress, but still it is a difficult.

Another possible reason is their food problem. Their food is limited to only one kind. What's that? Who knows? Yes, the bamboos. They don't eat anything else. But, unfortunately, it is reported that large area of bamboo groves in their habitat are in full bloom and died. Our Biologists are worried that we can not find enough food for pandas. Also, the giant pandas are big eaters. They always eat and eat, and for one day a panda can eat about 20-25 kilograms of bamboo leaves or bamboo shoots. This causes their digest problem.

Our city is not far from the habitat of pandas. It's about 7 hours' ride by bus. Here the climate, the environment is similar to that of their habitat. So it's a very good place for pandas. And altogether, we have 5 pandas in our zoo. But I'm not sure if we can see all of them today. This is because the pandas are wild animals. To keep them wild, every year they will be sent in turn to their habitat to live in natural environment for 3-6 months. If we are lucky enough we may see four of them or three of them.

OK, here we are. We'll get off here. And please stay here for a moment after getting off the bus. I'll go to get the admission tickets for our group.

Ladies and gentlemen, are you ready? Follow me please.

Sample Speech 2

Visiting the People's Great Hall of Chongqing

Keys to Introduction

1. General information.

Name, location, history, formation, usage.

2. Main features.

Unique architectural style, a combination of both ancient architectural art and modern technique.

Good morning, ladies and gentlemen.

Today we're going to visit the People's Great Hall of Chongqing, a symbol building of our city Chongqing. It's located in Yuzhong District, right in the downtown area, about ten minutes ride from our hotel.

The People's Great Hall of Chongqing is a very magnificent architecture. It has a history of 60 years. The construction of this building started in 1951 and was completed in 1955. It took us 4 years to complete it. Consisting of the main building and two wing buildings, the whole complex covers a total area of 66,000 square meters.

The main building is 65 meters tall with a ball-shaped cover. Inside is a big round hall, which is 46 meters in diameter, and 55 meters in net height, without a single pillar. The whole building is supported by the huge steel net on the top. The hall has four floors and it can hold 5, 000 people for conferences, concerts, drama performances, and other cultural activities. The two wing buildings are used as a hotel. It's a 3-star hotel and it is the first hotel to receive foreign visitors in our city.

The whole complex is in the style of ancients. [③] It looks like an ancient building. As you can see, the main part is an imitation of the Temple of Heaven in Beijing. The front part of the main building is an imitation of the Tian'an Men city tower. The two wing buildings are an imitation of the Forbidden City. Actually, it is not an ancient building but a modern one. It is made of steels and concrete.

It is a masterpiece of well combination of both ancient architectural art and modern technique. [④] And it plays an important part in China's architectural history. In 1982, in the book *The Comparative Architectural History*[⑤] by London University and the Royal Architects Association of Great Britain, 47 well-known Chinese architectures were included and introduced to the world, among which our Great Hall ranked the second (the first was the Temple of Heaven).

In front of the building, there's the people's square. Every morning or evening, many people come here for exercise (playing Taiji and dancing) and for relaxation.

Right across the square is the New Three Gorges Museum. In the museum, there is a huge model of the Dam Project and variety of cultural relics found in the three gorges area being displayed there and be shown to the public.

Now the Great Hall has become a well-known tourist attraction and it attracts a great number of domestic and foreign visitors coming for sightseeing.

OK, here we are. We'll first stay in the square for about 20 minutes for pictures. Then we'll get into the hall to have a look around. After that we'll move to the next spot.

Sample Speech 3

A Visit to the Ancient Town of Ciqikou

Keys to Introduction

1. General information.

Name (how it got its name), location.

2. Main features.

Its history—over 1,000 years;

Old houses—Diaojiaolou;

Old pebbled street;

The leisure life of the local people there—old teahouses.

Good morning, everyone. Now we are heading for the old town of Ciqikou. It's about 30 minutes' drive from our hotel. So I'd like to introduce you something about the old town. This old town is located right by the Jialing River northwest of Chongqing, not far from the city proper. So it is very convenient for the tourists to come for sightseeing. In ancient times, this town was rich in pottery and china production. It was also a busy port. Hence it was called Ciqikou which means in Chinese a port for shipping pottery products.

Legend has it that in the Ming Dynasty there was an emperor whose throne was usurped by his uncle. ⑥ He was afraid of being killed by his uncle, so he escaped from his palace to the small town and became a monk hiding himself in one of the temples there. You know, in ancient China the emperor was believed to be the dragon incarnate⑦, so this town was also called Longyin town—the dragon-hidden town.

This old town is well known for its pebbled street, old teahouses, and Diaojiaolou⑧. The so-called Diaojiaolou are the local style old houses with white walls and gray roofs supported by wooden stakes over the ground. It's very nice to walk around the old town enjoying the old houses and bargaining in the souvenir shops. There are many old teahouses with performance of Sichuan Opera. They are the best place for relaxation. Local people have their own folk customs. After work they would go to the teahouse drinking tea, tasting peanuts, sunflower seeds and dried thin sheets of bean curd, and chatting with each other. They live a very leisure life there.

Now many city dwellers would come here for weekends. Sitting in the old teahouse, sipping tea, enjoying the beautiful river view, and chatting or playing cards with friends, it will make you thoroughly relaxed.

Well, we'll just go there and have a guided walk through the town. We'll stay there for about 40 minutes.

OK, here we are.

Notes

① As we all know, all the dinosaurs have become extinct, while the giant pandas survived. 众所周知,恐龙已经灭绝,而大熊猫存活下来了。

② poor multiply capability 很低的繁殖能力

③ The whole complex is in the style of ancients. 整个建筑群呈古典风格。

④ It is a masterpiece of well combination of both ancient architectural art and modern technique. 它是融古代建筑艺术与现代建筑技术于一身的杰作。

⑤ *The Comparative Architectural History*《比较建筑史》(1982 年由伦敦大学和英国皇家建筑师协会联合编著出版的学术著作)

⑥ ... whose throne was usurped by his uncle. ……皇位被他的叔叔篡夺了。

⑦ ... in ancient China the emperor was believed to be the dragon incarnate.... ……在古代中国,皇帝被认为是龙的化身……

⑧ Diaojiaolou 吊脚楼

Words and Expressions

landscape *n.* 景观;风景
genesis *n.* 缘由;起因

comprehensive　　*adj.* 综合的;广泛的
embrace　　*v.* 环绕;环抱
boast　　*v.* (自豪地)拥有
inhabit　　*v.* 栖息;居住
dinosaur　　*n.* 恐龙
extinct　　*adj.* 灭绝的;绝种的
habitat　　*n.* (动物)栖息地
multiply　　*v.* 繁殖;繁育
digest　　*v.* 消化;吸收(食物)
admission　　*n.* 门票;入场费
architecture　　*n.* 建筑;建筑物
complex　　*n.* 建筑群
imitation　　*n.* 模仿;仿制品
concrete　　*n.* 混凝土

head for　　前往…
be in danger of extinction　　濒临灭绝;面临灭绝的危险
be in a family way　　怀孕
artificial insemination　　人工繁育;人工授精
be limited to　　限于…
in diameter　　直径
right across　　在对面

Assignments

1. Write a tour guide speech according to the following requirements.

A Visit to the Old Town of Ciqikou

Directions: Your speech should include the following points.

(1) Opening statement.

Including greetings, precautions, schedule and arrangements.

(2) Introduction.

A. General information:

Location, name (how it got its name).

B. Main features:

Its history—over 1,000 years;
Old houses—Diaojiaolou;
Old street—pebbled street;
Old teahouses—the leisure life of the local people there.

2. Translate the following into English.

(1) 我们现在前往西湖参观游览。
(2) 这里三面环水,状如半岛。
(3) 该景区由三部分组成,占地面积150平方千米。
(4) 整个建筑呈古代建筑风格,看起来雄伟壮观。
(5) 1999年,它被列为世界自然遗产。

In-class Practice

Role-play

Divide the class into two teams to role-play (local guide and guests), making an introduction to the following scenic spots:

(1) The Three Natural Bridges in Wulong.
(2) Chongqing—A City of Hot Springs.
(3) The Heavenly Pit and Earth-crack in Fengjie.

Broaden Your Mind

Ancient Diaoyu Castle

Standing on the top of the Diaoyu Hill east of Hechuan, the Ancient Diaoyu Castle is the best-preserved ancient battlefield site in China. In 1982, it was inscribed as one of the first batch of National Key Scenic and Historic Interest Areas by the State Council. In 1996, it was listed as one of the fourth batch of Unit of Cultural Relics under State Protection by the State Council. In 2012, it was included in the first batch of National Archaeological Park project list by China Cultural Heritage Administration.

In the 13th century, during the war between Song and Mongolia (Yuan Dynasty), in order to prevent the Mongolian Army from invading, Yujie, governor of Sichuan Province and magistrate of Chongqing, adopted the suggestion by the two brothers—Ranjin and Ranpu from Bozhou (today's Zunyi Guizhou Province) and constructed the castle on Diaoyu Hill, moving Hezhou Prefecture government and Shizhao County government onto the top of the hill, with troops stationed and food stocked in the castle as a defense for Chongqing.

From 1243 to 1279, soldiers and civilians of Hezhou of the Southern Song Dynasty, led by general Wang Jian and Zhang Jue, made full use of the strategic point of the castle and fought a bloody battle more than 200 fights against the Mongolian Army, the world's most powerful military force at that time and kept the war of resistance against Mongolia for 36 years. In 1259, Mongke Khan (Emperor Xianzhong of the Yuan Dynasty), who led his army fighting west smashing their way through Asia and Europe and was famed as "God's whip of punishment for crimes", was killed at the foot of Ancient Diaoyu Castle. The whole world was shocked.

Sites of military and living facilities of the Southern Song Dynasty still retain in the main scenic area covering a land of 2.5 square kilometers, such as the 8-kilometer-long city wall, 8 city gates, battery, navy pier, ordnance workshop, secret passage exit, barracks and military training field, pools and wells. There are a lot of places of historic interest and scenic beauty including the Fishing Stand, Suspended Sleeping Buddha of Tang Dynasty, Thousand-Buddha Cliff, Standing Statue of Maitreya, 800-year-old Osmanthus Tree, Tianquan Cave, Baodao Ridge, Three-tortoise Rock, Huguo Temple, Zhongyi Shrine, Three-Saint Cliff, and Eight Beautiful Vistas of Diaoyu Hill. There are also stone carvings and cliff inscriptions of chants by men of letters of the past ages such as Wen Tianxiang, Liu Kezhuang, Yang Shen, Chen Yi, Guo Moruo, Zhou Gucheng, Zhang Aiping, and Liu Baiyu, and by the high-ranking officials and officers of the Kuomintang such as Chiang Kai Shek, He Yingqin, and Zhang Zhizhong.

Main attractions include:

Huguo City Gate

Located on the second line of defense south of the castle, the Huguo City Gate is an important channel guarding the castle and connecting the castle to the outside. The city gate is in east-west direction leaning on the hill on the right and over steep cliffs on the left, having a plank road along the cliffs as its only access in the past time. The existing double-arched gate tunnel has been renovated in Ming and Qing Dynasties, on which is an inscription of "strategic point of Shu".

Fishing Stand

It is a huge abrupt rock overlooking the Jialing River, 11 meters in height, flat on top. On the stand there is a pair of pits which are about 1 meter long, shaped like a pair of footprints.

Sleeping Buddha

It is a huge statue of sleeping Buddha carved in Tang Dynasty. The statue of Buddha was carved in a hanging cliff, facing the south and back to the north, with its head to the west and feet to the east, exposing its chest and arms, with plump face, presenting dignified, kind and natural expression. It is a rare wonder that the sleeping Buddha in Ancient Diaoyu Castle is hovering in a hanging cliff.

Huoguo Temple

Huoguo Temple was first founded by the famous Buddhist monk namely Monk Stone of Hezhou in Tang Dynasty. In the 25th year in Shaoxing's reign in Southern Song Dynasty (in 1155), Tian Shaoqing, a military officer donated money for renovation, and over one hundred rooms and halls were built. In the second year in Dade's reign in Yuan Dynasty (in 1298), it was burnt in a war. In the seventh year in Hongzhi's reign in Ming dynasty (in 1494), it was reconstructed on its original site. At the turn of the Ming and Qing Dynasties, the temple was destroyed by war again. It was reconstructed in the fifth year in Yongzheng's reign in Qing Dynasty. The existing Huguo Temple is the legacy after two years renovation and reconstruction by the abbot monk Huizhi in the thirteenth year in Daoguang's reign in Qing Dynasty.

Unit 4 On-spot Guiding
现场导游

【内容导读】

本单元通过实例介绍英文现场导游的内容、要点、技巧及注意事项等内容。

【学习目标】

掌握英文现场导游的要点和技巧。

【学习要点】

现场导游讲解词的准备,现场导游常用口语句型。

Text

Skills of On-spot Guiding

When leading tourists on a site tour, the tour guide must deliver an on-spot tour commentary to the tourists, and introduce the scenic spots to them. For an on-spot tour commentary, the tour guide must first try to draw the guests' attention, then introduce a chosen list of key ideas or messages and extend them. The length of the tour commentary should be in accordance with the length of the tour or itinerary. And it must be correct, clear, making sense, sequential and logical.

In order to arouse their interest and deepen their impression, it is better to use simple words and speak in a humorous way. This can make your introduction natural, vivid, impressive, and convincing.

When making an introduction, the tour guide should choose an appropriate location and face the tourists. The tour guide should also pay attention to interaction between the guide and the guests, and be ready to answer or explain possible questions by the guests. But remember: don't argue with the tourist and don't pretend to know what you don't know.

Oral Skills

Useful Patterns for On-spot Guiding

Here we are. This is the West Lake.
Now we've come to the... (a scenic spot).
On the way up, it is the... (a scenic spot).

Please look at the right side / left side / in front of us.
Look, there is a pagoda on the right.

Watch out your steps. It's slippery here.
Mind your head.
Be careful.

The duration / time of sightseeing is 2 hours.
We'll stay here for 30 minutes.
You may have a look around / walk around.

I'll be waiting for you at the main entrance.
Please meet at the gate at 5 o'clock.
Please remember, our bus number is....

Here we go.
Let's on the bus.
Let's move.
If you are ready, we'll move to the next spot.

Sample Speech 1

Visiting the Temple of Guanyin

Ladies and gentlemen, now we have come to the Temple of Guanyin. Please look in front of us. There is a huge Buddha sculpture. As you can see, this Buddha sculpture was carved in a huge rock face, covering an area of 88 square meters. And it has many hands and each hand is in different gesture, and there is an eye in each hand. This is the thousand-handed and thousand-eyed Bodhisattva Guanyin[①].

"*Wow, it's marvelous!*"

Yes, really. Here's a question for you. Just guess, how many hands does this Guanyin have?

"*Er, let me see, the hands are arranged irregularly. It's very difficult to count. Several hundred, maybe?*"

"*About one thousand, I guess.*"

Actually, there are 847 hands and eyes in total.

"*Why the Buddha has so many hands and eyes? And what do the hands and eyes mean?*"

Well, in Chinese language, the word "thousand" means "many", not really one thousand. According to Buddhist Doctrine, here the "hand" is "helping hand", meaning that Guanyin is willing to offer a hand to those who need help. And the "eyes" refer to wisdom, meaning that Guanyin can see everything.[②] Here's a story about that.

You know, Buddhism originated from India. Legend has it that[③] in ancient India there was a king named King Miaozhuang who had three daughters. The youngest daughter was named Miaoshan. When she was very young, Miaoshan decided to go to a Buddhist temple, where there were 500 monks, to become a nun to practice Buddhism. Her father didn't agree and didn't allow her to go there, but she insisted on going to the temple. In order to prevent her from being a nun, the king ordered to kill the 500 monks. Then he had 500 running sores all over his body for the evil he did. He tried every medicine he could get to cure his sores, but it didn't work. One day, Buddha told him that only by taking a hand and an eye from his blood relations as the medicine could his sores be cured. But his first two daughters wouldn't like to give their hands and eyes to their father. In order to atone for her father's crime and to show her filial obedience[④], the third daughter Miaoshan said to Buddha that she was willing to contribute one of her hands and eyes to her father. After that her father got well. Buddha said to her, "You are a dutiful daughter and you are very kindhearted. You showed your mercy to other people. Since you have lost one hand and one eye, I'll give you a thousand hands and eyes in return, so that you can see everything and can give a hand to those who need help". Hence the thousand-handed and thousand-eyed Guanyin, also known as the Goddess of Mercy[⑤].

"*I have seen a quite different sculpture of Bodhisattva Guanyin, she has a baby in her arms. What's the difference between the two?*"

This is because each Bodhisattva has its own responsibility. According to Esoteric Buddhism, Guanyin is also responsible for birth, that is, to present a baby to those married couples. Thus Guanyin is also known as Mother Guanyin or Mother God⑥.

OK, let's move to the next spot.

Sample Speech 2

Visiting the Great Wall

Ladies and gentlemen, here we are at the foot of the Great Wall. So this is the famous wall. Please look up, the Great Wall runs all the way along the mountain ridges across the eastern half of China. Its length is about 6,000 kilometers. That's why we Chinese call it "Ten-thousand-li Long Wall".

"*Oh, what a marvelous sight! How high is it?*"

The average height of the wall is 7.5 meters. Please look at the towers on the wall spaced at equal distance from each other. They are beacon-fire towers. You know, the wall was constructed in ancient times to guard against invasion by the nomadic tribes from the north. When people found enemy troops approaching, they would send smoke signals from the tower as an alarm. When the guards in the neighboring tower saw the signals, they would do the same. In this manner, the signals would be sent to the capital.

"*What a striking idea!*"

Look, these steps will take us there. Let's go.

(A moment later) Now, we are here at the No. 4 Southern Tower, the summit of the wall at Badaling. As a Chinese saying goes, "If you fail to reach the Great Wall, you are not a true man"⑦. Today, we are all great men in climbing the Great Wall.

"*Oh, yeah! We've ascended the Great Wall of China at last. We are great men!*"

Now, please look into the distance, you can see that the Great Wall looks like a giant dragon and the mountain ranges are like a vast sea; the giant dragon seems to rise and fall, twisting and turning in the seething waves....⑧This view also make one feel so relaxed and happy.

OK, come on, ladies and gentlemen, let's take a group picture on the Great Wall.

Notes

① thousand-handed and thousand-eyed Bodhisattva Guanyin 千手千眼观音

② And the "eyes" refer to wisdom, meaning that Guanyin can see everything. "眼"表示智慧,指观音能洞悉世间一切。

③ legend has it that... 相传…; 据说…

④ In order to atone for her father's crime and to show her filial obedience... 为了替她的父亲赎罪和尽孝……

⑤ Goddess of Mercy 大慈大悲观音菩萨

⑥ Mother Guanyin or Mother God 送子观音或送子娘娘

⑦ "If you fail to reach the Great Wall, you are not a true man""不到长城非好汉"

⑧ ... the giant dragon seems to rise and fall, twisting and turning in the seething waves.... ……长城像一条巨龙在大海的波涛中起伏翻腾……

Words and Expressions

sequential	*adj.* 按顺序的;连贯的
logical	*adj.* 逻辑的;符合逻辑的
vivid	*adj.* 生动的
interaction	*n.* 互动
Buddha	*n.* 佛;佛陀
Bodhisattva	*n.* 菩萨
Buddhism	*n.* 佛教;释
Buddhist	*n.* 佛教徒
	adj. 佛教的;佛法的;佛教徒的
doctrine	*n.* 教义;教条
marvelous	*adj.* 不可思议的;了不起的;妙极的
striking	*adj.* 引人注目的;显著的
summit	*n.* 峰顶;顶点
seething	*adj.* 沸腾的;翻滚的
tour commentary	导游解说词
making sense	有意义

argue with 与…争论
running sore 脓疮
atone for crime 赎罪
filial obedience 孝;孝顺;孝心
beacon-fire tower 烽火台
nomadic tribe 游牧部落

Assignments

1. Write a tour commentary for on-spot guiding (in 500-1,000 words).
(1) Visiting Chaotianmen.
(2) Sightseeing the Kuimen Gate.
2. Translate the following into English.
(1) 我们要在这里停留30分钟,大家可以随意转转。
(2) 请大家往上看,有一尊巨大的佛像屹立在山顶上。
(3) 群山顶上的长城犹如一条巨龙在海中游动。
(4) 下午5点钟我会在景区大门处等候大家。
(5) 整个观音塑像雕刻在一面巨大的崖壁上,面积约80平方米。

In-class Practice

Role-play

Divide the class into two teams to role-play (local guide and guests) on-spot guiding according to the situations given below:
(1) Visiting Chaotianmen.
(2) Sightseeing the Kuimen Gate.

Broaden Your Mind

Yangtze River Gorges

Regarded as the nature's art gallery and wonderland, the Three Gorges are the most spectacular section of the Yangtze River and are famous for their breathtaking scenery, with Baidi City, Fengjie in Chongqing to the west end and Nanjin Pass of

Yichang to the east.

The Three Gorges, Qutang, Wu and Xiling, are total 192 km in length. Qutang Gorge, known for its magnificence and precipitousness, is only 8 km long. Wu Gorge, 44 km long, is famed for its deep valley and quiet beauty. Among the twelve peaks, the Goddess Peak is the most exquisite. Xiling Gorge, extending 66 km in length, was one of the most dangerous shoals full of turbulent currents and whirlpools. After the completion of the Dam project, it is now a quiet lake.

Along the Three Gorges, there are broad valleys, where the climate is mild and the soil fertile. These valleys are the main cultivated areas in the Three Gorges, where the county towns of Wushan, Badong and Zigui are located. In the autumn when the orange ripens, its sweet fragrance drifts to the boats on the river.

In addition to their scenic beauty, the Three Gorges are rich in water resources. They are the most ideal section of the Yangtze for building large water conservancy projects for the comprehensive exploitation of the river. The deep gorges and steep mountains on the banks of the river present superabundant potentials for power generation. The Three Gorges Dam Project has effectively got the torrential flow on the upper reaches under control and the middle and lower reaches are free from the threat of flood. Huge power generators send electricity to many parts of the country. The dangerous navigation channel is submerged in a placid lake. The Three Gorges presents an entirely different picture.

The beautiful landscape of the gorge region has given birth to a splendid culture. It is one of the birthplaces of the civilizations of China. The famous Daxi Culture, which originated here, has shed brilliant light on the civilizations in the long history. The valleys were once the battlefields during the period of the Three Kingdoms, where countless heroes displayed their prowess and talent. Besides, a great many well-known historical sites such as White Emperor City, Huangling Temple and Nanjin Pass, add charm to the landscape.

A sight-seeing tour of the Three Gorges and the historical and cultural monuments can be made only by boat. As a rule the excursion will commence in Chongqing and pass through Fuling, Fengdu, Wanzhou, Fengjie and Wushan to Yichang.

Unit 5 Translation of Tourism
旅游翻译

【内容导读】

本单元介绍旅游景观、景点名称及景区简介的英文翻译方法，包括直译法、意译法、音译法，并通过大量的案例分析，解读旅游翻译中常见的错误及导致翻译错误的原因。

【学习目标】

掌握正确的旅游翻译方法及各种翻译方法的要点。

【学习要点】

旅游翻译的直译法和意译法。

Text

在各种旅游景区、景点的参观游览票证、景区简介、景点名称与解说词、景区、景点路标路牌、酒店旅游手册以及旅游图册、旅游文献等出版物上，用英语传达的信息量越来越大。然而近年来，上述旅游翻译中不规范、不正确的翻译、中国式英语（Chinese-styled English）随处可见。一些旅游翻译错误百出，让人忍俊不禁。这不仅会对各景区、景点、旅游地乃至整个中国的对外形象造成严重的不利影响，也会对中国旅游业的健康发展带来极大的危害。准确、规范的旅游翻译对于树立景区的形象，吸引国外游客，促进中外交流具有十分重要的意义。掌握正确的旅游翻译方法，对于做好导游工作，提升导游服务质量也是非常必要的。

一、旅游景点的翻译方法 Translation of Landscapes

（一）直译法 Literal Translation

1. 概念。

直译法就是根据原文字面意思进行翻译，是指不仅忠实于原文内容，而且忠实于原文形式的翻译方法。

比如：

风景点（区） scenic spot / area

旅游吸引物 tourist attraction

森林公园 forest park

自然保护区 nature reserve

海洋公园 ocean park

停车场 parking lot

钓鱼台 fishing stand

鹰嘴峰 Eagle-mouthed Peak

南天门 South Heaven Gate

支柱产业 pillar industry

2. 翻译要点及问题分析。

我国著名的翻译家严复先生提出了“信、达、雅”三字翻译原则和标准。其中“信”是首要的，即忠实原文，忠实地传达原文的内容和风格。“翻译应该给出原作思想的完整复现”。

采用直译法进行旅游景点名称的翻译时，要切忌：

(1)生硬直译，简单对应，信息传递不准确、不完整。

例如，“中国国家重点风景名胜区”，有人将其对应译为 National Park(国家公园)或 National Park of China(中国国家公园)，这种英译是不太准确的。

这是因为，国家公园最早出现在美国，是一种国家天然公园，具有相对大面积的区域(不少于10平方公里)，区内具有自然原野景观、原生动植物群、一种或几种特殊的生态体系，有国家代表性，且未经人类开发、聚居或开发建设之地，在保护自然的前提下仅准许游客在特殊的情况下进入一定范围，作为科研、教育、旅游与启智资源的园地，实为自然露天博物馆或自然保护区。风景名胜区则是指具有自然景观、人文景观和它们所处的环境，以及与之密切关联的民俗风情等风景名胜资源集中、环境优美，具有一定规模和游览条件，经县级以上人民政府审定命名、划定范围，可供人们游览、休憩和进行科学、文化活动的地区。

由于社会制度、历史文化背景的不同，两者在概念和命名上均有一些差异。为了表现这一差异，忠实原文，“中国国家重点风景名胜区”的英译应当译为：“China National Key Scenic and Historic Interest Area”才是比较准确的。

另外，也有一些出版物或景区游览手册，将“中国国家重点风景名胜区”译为：“Important Scenic Spot of China”“China National Scenic Spot”“State Scenic Area of China”.

这些译法所表述的含义是不完整的。Scenic Spot 或 Scenic Area 是指风景点、风景区。尽管风景名胜区常被简称为风景区，但严格意义上风景区和风景名胜区二者是不相同的。风景名胜区内包括有风景资源和名胜资源，并非只是一般风景资源集中的地域，而在风景区内，则不一定有名胜资源。因此，上述译文所传达的信息是不准确的，至少是不完整的。

（2）望文生义，内涵把握不准确，导致信息传达错误。

翻译需要译者对原文的意思包括其内涵做充分、正确的了解和把握，这是译文表述的前提。由于译者对旅游业不熟悉，尤其在景区、景点名称的翻译中，对景区、景点的历史、内容、性质、特征、特色等不甚了解，对其内涵把握不准确，或者由于自身的文化底蕴不够，往往片面理解词义，从而导致旅游翻译中望文生义的翻译现象频繁出现。

如在《重庆国家级旅游风景区图典——缙云山·北温泉·钓鱼城》一书中，“钓鱼城”就被译者根据字面意思译为“Fishing City”。

钓鱼城是重庆合川境内的一处国家重点风景名胜区（缙云山·北温泉·钓鱼城风景名胜区的重要组成部分）和国家重点文物保护单位。公元13世纪，蒙古军队入侵中原，为抵御蒙古铁骑的侵犯，当地军民在位于嘉陵江边的陡峭山崖之上修筑堡垒等城防工事，作为保卫重庆的一道屏障。因该山形状似鱼形，故名“鱼山”。山上有一巨石，相传为洪荒时代巨人神在此持竿向江中钓鱼以救灾民，该山又称“钓鱼山”，该城防工事也就得名“钓鱼城”。

显然，这里的“城”，并非城市，实应为一军事要塞的古城堡。将其译为Fishing City是不恰当的，其所传达的信息是不准确的，游客不能从这一译文名称准确了解该景区的性质和特色。应将其译为“Ancient Diaoyu Castle”才恰如其分。

同样的道理，金佛山旅游简介将其景区内的景点“南宋古战场——龙岩城”译为“Ruins of Ancient Battlefield—Longyan City”也是不恰当的。应该译为：“Ancient Battlefield Site of the Southern Song Dynasty—Longyan Castle”.

下面的几则望文生义的译文更是贻笑大方：

一是金佛山旅游简介中一景观名称“金山烟雨”，其英文译文“Smoking Rain of Jinshan”；

二是四川蒲江朝阳湖景点示意图中将景区“大门”译为“Big Door”；

三是四川泸州尧坝古镇一方向指示牌“出口”，其英文译文“Export”。

这里的“烟雨”是指“蒙蒙细雨”或“雨雾”，并非“烟雾”；大门也不是指

"巨大的门",而应是指景区入口;"出口"不是商品货物的出口,而是出入古镇的出入口。

上述译文应分别译为:

Golden Mountain in Misty Rain;

Main Entrance;

Exit.

3. 知识性错误。

旅游翻译与其他翻译一样,并不是简单语言的对应转换,它还涉及多学科知识内容。比如,风景名胜区的旅游简介、景区景点名称等的翻译,就涉及社会、历史、文化、地理、宗教、民俗、建筑、艺术,甚至生物学、动植物学、生态学、考古学等多种学科知识,译者除应具有扎实的语言功底外,还应具备广博的多学科知识,至少应对上述学科知识有一个基本的了解。否则,翻译出来的译文就可能不准确,甚至闹出笑话。

如《重庆国家级旅游风景区图典——缙云山 · 北温泉 · 钓鱼城》一书第10页中就有这样一段译文:

"The scenic area includes North Hot Spring Park, Fishing City in Hechuan County, Yuejiang River, Hot Spring Valley near Jialing River flowing from Beibei to Hechuan County, ..."

该译文中所列出的 Yuejiang River 和 Hot Spring Valley 在何处,查遍了能找到的该地区的地图也找不到。此外,Beibei 这个小城明明在 Jialing River 的下游,而 Hechuan 在 Beibei 的上游,怎么 Jialing River 又从 Beibei 流向 Hechuan了呢?

对照该文的中文原文:"景区不限于缙云山,还包括缙云山下的北温泉,合川的钓鱼城,以及北碚至合川之间嘉陵江段的山岳江河、温泉峡谷(指温汤峡,笔者注)……" 原来该文译者将原文中的"山岳江河"割裂开来理解为"岳江河",将"北碚至合川之间嘉陵江段"想当然地认为嘉陵江从北碚流向合川,以致出现上述错误。

显然,这段文字的译文应为"The scenic area also includes the North Hot Spring at the foot of the Jinyun Mountain, the Ancient Diaoyu Castle in Hechuan as well as the mountains, streams, springs, and the Wentang Gorge in the section of the Jialing River between Beibei and Hechuan."

(二)意译法 Free Translation

1. 概念。

意译法是指忠实于原文内容,又不拘泥于原文结构形式与修辞手法的翻译方法。其以信息的传递为第一位。

2. 翻译要点。

由于文化的差异,汉语言中的某些表达在翻译中确实存在着不可译性。但只要注意对景点名称内涵的把握,采用意译法或加注和释义法,是基本可以处理和解决文化差异问题的。如:

太和殿 Hall of Supreme Harmony / Hall of Grand Harmony

烟霞洞 Cave of Morning Mist and Sunset Glow

一字城墙 City Wall Stringing out in a Single Line

嘉陵萦带 Winding Satin Belt of the Jialing River

赤壁文光 Light of Buddha on the Red Cliff

五花石街 Pebbled street

斗拱结构 A system of brackets inserted between the top of a column and a crossbeam

牌楼 Decorated Archway

牌坊 Memorial Archway

四合院 Courtyard with houses on the four sides; Chinese courtyard houses

西安古称长安。可译为:

Xi'an was called Chang'an (everlasting peace) in ancient times.

秦始皇兵马俑一号坑呈长方形,二号坑呈曲尺形,三号坑呈"凹"字形。三个坑呈"品"字形排列。可译为:

Pit No. 1 of Emperor Qin Shihuang's terra cotta warriors and horses is oblong in shape. Pit No. 2 is L-shaped and No. 3 is U-shaped. The three pits are arranged in a triangle.

(三)音译法 Transliteration

翻译人名、地名或一些具有很强的中国文化特色且不被国外读者所熟悉的东西时,可以通过视角转换或"文化借用"的方法直接音译。如:

太极 Taiji

饺子 Jiaozi

豆腐 Toufu

豫园 Yuyuan Garden

护国寺 Huguo Temple

峨眉山 Emei Mountain

但是，如果一篇译文中过多地出现汉语拼音替代翻译的现象，就难以做到信息的准确传递，使读者尤其是国外读者难以理解，从而降低译文的可读性和译文的质量。

有的旅游翻译中由于用词错误或不规范，或者由于语句错误，使得译文晦涩难懂，信息传达错误，降低了景区、景点及旅游地的品位。

《泰山》一书中，有这样一段译文：

"Mt. Tai was designated as an important scenic spot of China in 1982. It was entered in the World Natural and Cultural Heritage List by UNESCO in 1987."

这段译文中，译者选用了 enter 一词，用作及物动词，意为"把…记入；登录"，用在 enter sth. in ... 结构中，后面常跟如 list, catalogue, account 等词。如：

enter a book in a catalogue 把书登入图书目录

enter an item in an account 把一笔账记入账目

因此，上面这则译文的后一句应译为：

"It was entered in the *World Natural and Cultural Heritage List* by UNESCO in 1987."

或改译为：

"It was inscribed as a *World Natural and Cultural Heritage* by UNESCO in 1987."

二、景点简介翻译 Translation of the Brief Introduction to Scenic Spots

景点简介内容主要涉及景区景点名称、地理方位、面积大小、景观描述、特色，以及景区景点的头衔、荣誉、称号等。

Useful patterns for translation:

1. 表示景点地理方位。

be located (situated) on / in / by / at...

lie in / by / at...

stand in / by / at...

tower in / by / at...

be surrounded by... on three sides

e. g., The scenic area is located in the middle section of the Longbao Mountain on the northern bank of the Yangtze River.

Towering in the Central Plain in Shandong Province, Mount Taishan is known as the most easterly sacred mountain.

It is surrounded by water (by the sea) on three sides.

2. 表示景区的构成与占地面积。

cover an area (a land) of . . . square kilometers

consist of . . . and cover an area of. . .

e. g. , It consists of five parts and covers an area of 129 square kilometers.

Consisting of five parts, the scenic area covers a land of 50 square kilometers.

3. 表示景点的特色。

feature. . .

be typical of . . .

be characterized by. . .

be famous (well-known) for . . . / as . . .

e. g. , It features Karst landform.

The scenic area is typical of Karst landform.

It is characterized by Karst landform.

Simian Mountain is famous for its Danxia landform and waterfalls.

4. 表示景点拥有的资源。

there be. . .

boast

be rich in. . .

e. g. , There are 36 peaks, 42 caves and 9 streams in the scenic area.

Boasting 72 temples, over 600 monks and nuns, it is known as one of the Four Famous Buddhist Mountains in China.

It is rich in variety of precious wild animals and plants, hence it enjoys the fame as the Treasure House of Greenery.

5. 表示景点的名誉/称号/名声等。

be known as. . .

be famous for. . .

be famed as. . .

be noted for. . .

enjoy the fame as. . .

e. g. , The Yangtze River Gorges is known as one of the Top Ten Scenic and Historic Interest Areas in China.

Jiu Zhai Gou enjoys the name as the Fairyland.

Shanhaiguan Pass is famed as the No. 1 Pass under the Heaven.

6. 景物景观的描述。

thunderous sound 轰鸣如雷

tremendous momentum 气势磅礴

wonderful and marvelous sight 美妙的奇观;壮观的景象

charming scenery 景色迷人

present a magnificent view 呈现出壮观的景色

with lush green forests, fragrant flowers, singing birds, and bubbling streams

树木苍翠,花香袭人,鸟语婉转,流水潺潺

Flowers are in full bloom. 花儿竞相开放。

e. g. , 苍山巍峨挺拔,山顶终年积雪,山麓四季常青。

The mountain peak towers aloft, with the top snow-capped perennially, and vegetation and trees at the foot perpetually green and refreshing.

溪流飞瀑穿石,清碧澄澈,四季不绝。

The stream rushes downhill against rocks, forming ponds here and there, crystal clear all year round.

天坑风景区位于重庆奉节县境内,是一个直径626米、深662米的漏斗形天然大坑。天坑属典型的喀斯特地貌,坑内悬崖绝壁,奇特壮观;坑外草木葱翠,景色迷人。

Tiankeng (the Heavenly Pit) scenic area, located in Fengjie County, Chongqing, is a big funnel-shaped natural doline which is 626 meters in diameter and 662 meters in depth. It is typical of the Karst landform. With steep cliffs inside, it presents a wonderful and marvelous sight, while outside the pit is the charming scenery of green.

Words and Expressions

literal	*adj.* 字面的;原意的
transliteration	*n.* 音译
pebble	*n.* 卵石
	v. 用卵石铺
archway	*n.* 牌楼;拱门
sacred	*adj.* 神圣的;宗教的

aloft	*adv.* 在空中;在高处
snow-capped	*adj.* 积雪盖顶的
doline	*n.* 落水洞;石灰坑

National Park	国家公园
Light of Buddha	佛光
Karst landform	喀斯特地貌
Danxia landform	丹霞地貌
be in full bloom	盛开

Four Famous Buddhist Mountains in China 中国四大佛教名山

Top Ten Scenic and Historic Interest Areas in China 中国十大风景名胜区

Assignments

Translate the following into English.

道人拜月	秀峰	倒挂玉荷	清凉世界	仙人台
观音听琵琶	春色	鹰嘴岩	天上玉屏	卧佛
杜甫草堂	海天佛国——普陀山			

青龙瀑布景区位于重庆万州龙宝山中部,长江北岸,面积35平方公里。青龙瀑布因青龙河而得名。瀑布高65米,宽105米,水声轰鸣如雷,水花飞溅如雨,气势磅礴。

In-class Practice

Divide the class into groups to have a discussion about the English translation of the following:

(1) 浪漫的温泉之都——重庆。

(2) 重庆,非去不可。

Broaden Your Mind

Ancient Town of Laitan

The Ancient Town of Laitan is located about 28 kilometers northeast of Hechuan Chongqing. Surrounded by mountains and water, boasting beautiful landscapes, a long history and splendid culture, it is one of the first batch of Famous Historical and Cultural Towns of China, Unit of Cultural Relics under State Protection, National AAA level Tourist Scenic Area, and one of the Most Beautiful Villages and Small Towns in China.

The Ancient Town of Laitan, established in Song Dynasty, is enclosed by steep cliffs in three sides, and is strategically located and difficult of access. In the old town, wooden structured small houses with grey roofs built in Ming and Qing Dynasties are scattered randomly over the mountain slopes. Stone-paved streets, narrow and crooked, but in a proper size, together with the inner yards on both sides, are of classic elegance, giving visitors a feeling of being in a cordial and quiet mountain village. The barbican entrance to the old town(瓮城), which was built in the first year in emperor Tongzhi's reign in Qing Dynasty, with four gates and eight gateways, has the advantage of feints and ambushes in resisting the enemy. The Wenchang Shrine, built in Qing Dynasty, is still well-preserved. The woodcut and relief sculptures on the outer rails of the ancient drama stage are acclaimed as the acme of perfection. In addition, there are also remains of Huilong Temple and Zhangye Shrine, and beautiful tales of the nine Taoist temples and eighteen Buddhist temples.

Main attractions in the old town include:

Er'fo Buddhist Temple

The Er'fo Temple in the old town, which was first built in Tang Dynasty and prosperous in Song Dynasty, consists of upper and lower halls. The lower hall is located in the Jiufeng Mountain. The two-storey hall, built against the mountain cliffs, has arch eaves and rising wings. More than 1700 stone sculptures in different shapes are vivid and lifelike. They are the crystallization of the wisdom of the laboring people of the Tang and Song Dynasties, the typical representative works of the art of Chinese stone carvings in its third high tide period. The lower hall itself is the largest Buddhist rite of the Zen Buddhism Sect, a Unit of Cultural Relics under State Protection. The upper hall lies on the top of the Jiufeng Mountain. Being on a grand scale, and having strong religious atmosphere, it is magnificent. And the hollowed-out stone carvings of the arch gate are carved elegantly. Boasting 42 shrines, 1700 stone sculptures, the Er'fo Temple is the largest site of statues of Zen Buddhism Sect in China. The statue of Shakya Muni, 12.5 meters in height, is the largest one in the temple and one of the famous statues of Buddha in China.

Old Streets

The Old Streets, facing the Qujiang River in the east and bounded by steep cliffs in the south and north, consist of two streets and two alleys such as Shuncheng Street, Huilong Street, and Er'fo Lane. The main body of the Old Streets still maintain the architectural style of the Ming and Qing Dynasties. Wooden structured residential buildings on both sides of the street are well-proportioned, showing us the architecture style of ancient Bayu mountainous residences in east Sichuan province.

Barbican Entrance to the Old Town

The Barbican Entrance to the Old Town was built in the first year in emperor Tongzhi's reign in Qing Dynasty (in 1862). It was a fortification constructed to prevent the intrusion of the Taiping army and the peasant uprising at that time. It is currently the only well-preserved ancient military defensive fortress building in Chongqing and it is of great artistic value and appreciation value.

Wen Chang Shrine

Built in the third year in emperor Xianfeng's reign in Qing Dynasty, the Wen-Chang Shrine consists of the Hall of Confucius, ancient Drama Stage, the East and West Corridors, and covers an area of 6 Mu. Facing the south, with upturned eaves, it is a courtyard with wooden structured buildings on four sides. On the outer rails of the ancient drama stage are woodcut and relief sculptures of opera stories of the Three Kingdoms Period, elegantly and exquisitely carved, they are rare wooden treasures.

Wandering in the old town of Laitan and lingering among the religious atmosphere and the beautiful mountain views, one can feel carefree and leisurely, and have infinite pleasure.

Unit 6　Having a Group Dinner
团队用餐

【内容导读】

本单元介绍安排旅游团队用餐的流程，包括用餐安排、点菜、为客服务、结账等环节内容，以及各环节常用用语和句型；重点介绍中餐菜名的英文翻译方法及菜品介绍的方法与常用句型。

【学习目标】

掌握中餐菜名的英文翻译方法及菜品介绍的方法与常用句型。

【学习要点】

中餐菜名的英文翻译及菜品介绍方法。

Text

Arrangement of Group Dinner

Meal is one of the basic elements of tourist activities. Every year millions of people go to other countries to see beautiful scenery, historical sites, local customs, and at the same time, to eat exotic food. To taste foreign food is not only one of the important motivations for tourists to travel around the world, but also a special experience for tourists, especially for gourmands. ① Generally, when foreign visitors on a package tour come to China, a group dinner is arranged for them to try Chinese food, and the local specialties.

Oral Skills

Ⅰ. Process of Having a Group Dinner

Procedure and Useful Patterns

Step 1　Arrange a group dinner.

When arranging a group dinner, the tour guide needs to explain the reason for such a group dinner, and tell the guests the time and place for the group dinner.

You may use the following useful patterns:

Well, some of you guys told me that you would like to taste the local food. You know, to taste foreign food is one of the motivations for tourists to travel around the world. It's also a special experience for you. So we'll have a group dinner this evening.

Well, today I specially arrange a real Chinese dinner for you to get a special experience.

Well, today is the birthday of ... in this group. We'll have a celebration for that this evening. So I arranged a group dinner for you to share his / her happiness. I think it will be a very interesting experience for you.

I've made a reservation with one of the local restaurants for the group dinner. We'll go there at 6:30 p. m. It's not far from the hotel within five minutes walk. I'll be waiting for you at 6:30 p. m. in the lobby, OK?

Step 2 Seat the guests at the restaurant.

You may use the following useful patterns:

OK, here we are at the ... Restaurant. This way please.

Well, this table is for us / the two tables are for us.

Take a seat please. / Be seated please. / Take your seat as you like. / Please be seated.

Each table is for 8 people.

Step 3 Order dishes for the group.

Before ordering dishes for the group, you'd better ask whether there are any vegetarians or Muslim people in the tour group, and ask the tourists if they are severely allergic to any foods or M. S. G. ② Remember that most of the Western people don't eat the internal organs of animals such as intestines, livers, hearts, stomach, or blood, and paws. They also don't like to eat the food with too many bones.

You may use the following useful patterns:

Are there any vegetarians or Muslim in this group?

Is there anyone who is allergic to anything?

So what would you like to have?

Can I recommend some local dishes to you?

I've ordered beef, shrimp, pork, Jiaozi, Toufu and some fresh green vegetables for you, and an egg custard for the baby. Will this be OK?

If you would like to try...?

Step 4 Serve the guests.

You may use the following useful patterns:

This is ... (dish).... It is made of ... (ingredients).... It is ... (taste).... Just have a try.

Shall I ask the waitress to bring you a knife and fork?

Will you have a high chair for your baby?

One more beer?

How is the food?

I' m very glad that you enjoyed it.

Step 5 Bill.

You may use the following useful patterns:

Well, the group dinner is included in the price you paid for this package tour, so, you don' t need to pay.

Well, for the bill, we' ll just share the bill for this group dinner.

The total for this dinner is 280 *RMB, and we got* 8 *people, so it' s* 35 *RMB for each person, only for the adult, not for the baby.*

I' ve paid / cleared the bill just now. You just pay me later on. OK?

Ⅱ. Translation of Chinese Dishes

1. Cooking process.

fry;fried (cook in much fat / oil) 炸,炒

stir-fried 炒,爆炒

cook;cooked (at the table, like hot pot)煮

boil;boiled (cook in water) 煮

poach;poached (by cracking the shell)煮

smoke;smoked 熏

bake;baked (by dry heat in an oven) 烘烤

baked in salt 盐焗

roast;roasted (over a fire) 烤

grill;grilled (on a gridiron over great heat) 烧烤

marinate; marinated 腌制,卤制
seasoned with soy sauce 酱制
sautee; sauteed (quick fry in little fat) 煎
braise; braised (cook slowly in a covered pot in little liquid) 焖,煨,烩
braised in brown sauce 红烧
steam; steamed 蒸
steamed with rice flour 粉蒸
stew; stewed (cook slowly in liquid in a container) 炖

2. Cutting.
slice; sliced 片
shred; shredded 丝
mince; minced 颗粒、碎粒
dice; diced 丁

3. Different tastes.
spicy / hot 辣
peppery 胡椒味的,麻味的
salty / salted 咸味的
bitter 苦味的
sour 酸味的
sweet 甜味的
sweet-and-sour 糖醋味的
sour-and-hot 酸辣味的
fish-flavored 鱼香味
multi-flavored 怪味
Home-made 家常味
strong-flavored 味道很大,浓,强烈的
plain-flavored 味道平和的
mild / light 清淡的
tender 嫩的
delicious / very tasty 美味的,可口的

一、直译法 Literal Translation

1. 直接按中文菜名译出其意,并可对其含义进行适当补充,如:
叫花鸡 Beggar's Chicken
龙虎斗 Battle Between Dragon and Tiger(Stewed Snake and Cat's Meat)

春卷 Spring Rolls

四喜丸子 Four-Joy Meatballs (Meatballs Braised with Brown Sauce)

有些中国菜名十分生动形象,在采用直译法翻译这些菜名时,切忌望文生义,生硬直译。必须搞清楚这些菜肴的主料、配料和制作方法,否则就会闹笑话。

如:

"童子鸡",有人把它翻译成:Chicken Without Sexual Life(还没有过性生活的鸡)

"夫妻肺片"翻译成:Husband and Wife Lung Slice(丈夫和妻子的肺切片)

实际上,童子鸡就是小嫩鸡,而不是老鸡。夫妻肺片,实际上是猪肺的切片。因此,这两道菜名可以翻译成:Young Chicken 或 Young Adult Chicken 或 Teen Chicken;Sliced Pork Lungs in Chili Sauce.

2. 根据成菜的制作方法和原材料(主料)进行翻译,如:

烤鸭 Roasted Duck

炸鸡 Fried Chicken

铁扒猪排 Grilled Pork Chop

椒盐猪排 Dried Fried Pork Chop

软炸鱼块 Soft-fried Fish Chips

炒鸡蛋 Scrambled Eggs

炒腰花 Sauteed Kidney

红烧羊肉 Braised Mutton in Brown Sauce

清蒸鳜鱼 Steamed Mandarin Fish

烤羊肉串 Grilled Mutton

土豆泥 Mashed Potatoes

醋熘鱼卷 Fish Rolls in Sour Sauce

粉蒸肉 Steamed Pork with Rice Flour

卤水鹅头 Marinated Goose Heads

酱牛肉 Sliced Beef in Soy Sauce

盐焗鸡 Baked Chicken in Salt

3. 根据菜品的原料,以主料+(with/and)辅料的结构进行翻译,如:

宫保肉丁 Diced Pork with Peanuts

番茄鸡蛋汤 Tomato and Egg Soup

奶油蘑菇汤 Mushroom Soup with Cream

番茄虾仁 Shrimps with Tomatoes

鸡丝烩鱼翅 Shark's Fin and Shredded Chicken

蚝油西兰花 Broccoli with Oyster Sauce

香菇菜心 Cabbage Heart with Mushroom

虾仁豆腐 Bean Curd with Shrimp

榨菜肉丝 Shredded Pork with Pickled Tuber Mustard

4. 根据菜品制作方法和原材料相结合的方法进行翻译，如：

葱爆羊肉 Stir-fried Mutton with Green Scallion

红烧牛肉 Braised Beef in Brown Sauce

芙蓉蟹片 Deep-fried Crabmeat Slices and Egg-white

香菇鸭 Braised Duck with Mushroom

番茄炒鸡蛋 Stir-fried Eggs with Tomatoes

姜爆鸭子 Stir-fried Duck with Ginger

5. 根据成菜的不同口味进行翻译，如：

糖醋里脊（古老肉）Sweet-and-sour Pork

辣子肉丁 Spiced Diced Pork

辣子鸡 Spicy Chicken

鱼香肉丝 Fish-flavored Shredded Pork

怪味鸡 Multi-flavored Chicken

酸辣汤 Sour-and-hot Soup

陈皮兔丁 Diced Rabbit Meat with Tangerine Flavor

二、意译法 Free Translation

中国菜有相当一部分的命名是“写意”的。这类菜名往往不出现原料及烹调方法，不适宜采用直译法，而需要采用意译法，即需要把握菜名的内涵，通过释义或加注方法进行翻译。如：

龙凤会（这里“龙”指蛇，“凤”指鸡）Stewed Snake and Chicken

红烧狮子头（“狮子头”就是肉丸）Braised Meat Ball in Brown Sauce

回锅肉 Twice-cooked Pork Slices in Hot Sauce / Boiled and Fried Pork Slices

珍珠丸子 Meat Balls in Clear Soup

三、音译法 Transliteration

采用中国菜名的汉语拼音，即通过视角转换或“文化借用”的方法直接音译。对某些使用汉语拼音不能明白的菜名，还可以通过加注解释的方法。如：

宫保鸡丁 Kongpao Chicken

豆腐 Toufu

饺子 Jiaozi

馄饨，云吞 Hutun / Yuntu（Mini jiaozi served in soup）

佛跳墙 Fotiaoqiang—Steamed Abalone with Fish Maw in Broth（lured by its delicious aroma even the Buddha jumped over the wall to eat this dish）

鱼香肉丝 Yu-shiang Shredded Pork

东坡肉 Dongpo Braised Pork

Ⅲ. Introducing a Chinese Dish

1. 介绍菜品名称及来历。

This is ...（name of the dish）.

2. 介绍菜品制作方法和原料（主料、配料）。

It is made of ...（cooking process and ingredients）.

3. 介绍成菜后的味道类型。

It is ...（taste of the dish）.

4. 请客人品尝。

Just have a try.

Sample

麻婆豆腐

This is Mapo Toufu. Mapo refers to an old lady with a pockmarked face③. Toufu means bean curd. It is sautéed bean curd with garlic, minced beef in chili sauce（or hot pepper）. It is said that the red-hot bean curd was invented by a pockmarked woman, hence it is named as Mapo Bean Curd.

Notes

① To taste foreign food is not only one of the important motivations for tourists to travel around the world, but also a special experience for tourists, especially for gourmands. 品尝外国食物不仅是旅游者周游世界的重要动机之一，对旅游者尤其对美食家而言，也是一种特别的体验。

② ... and ask the tourists if they are severely allergic to any foods or MSG. 询问游客中是否有人对某种食物或味精过敏。

③ Mapo refers to an old lady with a pockmarked face. 麻婆是指脸上长有麻子的老太婆。

Words and Expressions

exotic　　*adj.* 奇异的，异乎寻常的；异国的

motivation	*n.* 动机
gourmand	*n.* 美食家
specialty	*n.* 特产
vegetarian	*n.* 素食者
allergic	*adj.* 过敏的
pockmark	*n.* 麻子;痘痕
ingredient	*n.* 原料
sauce	*n.* 调味汁;酱汁
aroma	*n.* 香味;气味
chili	*n.* 辣椒
pepper	*n.* 胡椒;花椒
garlic	*n.* 大蒜
salt	*n.* 盐
vinegar	*n.* 醋
spices	*n.* 香料
aniseed	*n.* 茴香(八角)
Muslim	*n.* 穆斯林 *adj.* 穆斯林的

MSG (Monosodium Glutamate)	味精
egg custard	蛋羹;蒸鸡蛋
high chair	(小孩吃饭用的)高脚椅子
Sesame oil	芝麻油
Duck intestines	鸭肠
Ox Maw	毛肚

Assignments

1. Translate the following into English.

青椒肉丝	冬菇菜心	红烧肘子	白斩鸡	熘肝尖
金钱鱼肚	海鲜火锅	糖醋鱼	樟茶鸭	水煮鱼

2. Write a short passage to introduce the following dishes.

(1) 宫保鸡丁 Kongpao Chicken

(2) 回锅肉 Twice-cooked Pork

In-class Practice

Role-play

Divide the class into groups to role-play "arranging the guests to have hot pot". You need to give a brief introduction to the hot pot, including:

What is hot pot?

Why do the local people eat hot pot?

How to eat hot pot?

Broaden Your Mind

Chinese Food

Food has a special meaning to the Chinese people. The "waste not, want not" ethos means that a surprising range and variety of plants and animals, and every part of a plant or animal is used. This has given rise to a remarkable diversity in regional cuisine, but to Westerners it can be overwhelming—surprising, fantastic, delicious, horrifying or disgusting—but above all, different.

China can be divided into many geographical areas, and each area has a distinct style of cooking. The ingredients used in the food are based on the natural agricultural products of the region. In Northern China, for example, wheat is eaten more than rice as a staple food. Food using wheat as its main ingredient, such as noodles and dumplings is prevalent there. China's Southern cuisine uses far more rice, with such staples as rice noodles and Zongzi—sticky rice wrapped in leaves. Southern food is typically spicier, and many minorities eat chilies every day.

Sichuan Cuisine

Sichuan Cuisine is the most widely served cuisine in China. Sichuan Cuisine wins universal praise for its hotness, sourness and numbness it produces, which are rare in other regional cuisines. These together sums up the unique flavor of Chuan Cuisine, which enjoys a good reputation as a cuisine that is "one dish with one flavor and one hundred dishes with one hundred flavors". Its cooking methods include baking, sautéing, dry-sautéing and steaming. Chuan Cuisine has good combinations of flavors and often has thick gravy.

Although, Chuan Cuisine is served at every corner of the world, the most authentic

Sichuan food is still to be found at its hometowns: Chengdu and Chongqing.

Classic Sichuan dishes are Mapo Bean Curd (Mapo Toufu), Spicy Diced Chicken (Kongpao Chicken), Sliced Pork Lungs in Chili Sauce, Hot Pot, and Twice-cooked Pork.

Cantonese Cuisine

Cantonese Cuisine, also known as Yue Cuisine, is the culinary style of Guangdong Province. This particular type of Chinese food has been popularized by Chinese restaurants around the world as the majority of those who set up these restaurants were of Cantonese origin.

Guangdong dishes are characterized by their tender and slightly sweet taste. Sauces are a crucial seasoning in Guangdong cuisine. Classic Cantonese sauces are light and mellow. The most widely used sauces in Guangdong Cuisine include: hoisin sauce, oyster sauce, plum sauce and sweet and sour sauce. Other ingredients popular in Guangdong Cuisine include spring onions, sugar, salt, soya bean products, rice wine, corn starch, vinegar and sesame oil. Garlic is used heavily in some dishes, especially those in which internal organs, such as entrails, may emit unpleasant odors. Ginger, chili peppers, five-spice powder, powdered white pepper, star anise and a few other spices are used, but often sparingly.

The raw materials for Guangdong Cuisine are very plentiful. Things that are rarely eaten or rarely seen on Western tables are commonly used in Guangdong dishes. Snake, cat and pangolin (scaly anteater) are considered by the Cantonese people to be most delicious food.

In contrast to the fast-fried cooking method of Sichuan dishes, Guangdong people prefer to braise, stew and saute their food. These cooking methods aim to preserve the flavor of the dishes. Classic Cantonese dishes are Dry-Fried Beef and Noodles(干炒牛河), White Cut Chicken(白切鸡), Barbequed Pork (Char Siu)(叉烧).

Lu Cuisine

Lu Cuisine, also called Shandong Cuisine, is originated from the native cooking styles of East China's Shandong Province. It is the most prevalent distinct regional cuisine in China, popular through out Beijing, Tianjin and Northeast China.

Lu Cuisine is more inclined to keep the freshness of ingredients than other cuisines and fond of salt flavor, featured with tender, savory and crisp. It is particular about making soup.

Seafood is the most notable ingredient of Lu Cuisine as Shandong is a costal province, including scallops, prawns, clams, sea cucumbers, and squid, which are all local ingredients of exemplary quality. Besides seafood, corn, peanuts, grains such as small grains, millet, wheat, oat and barley, and staple vegetables of Shandong province including potatoes, tomatoes, cabbages, mushrooms, onions, garlic and eggplants.

There are over thirty cooking techniques applied in Lu Cuisine, among which Bao technique (quick-fry) and Pa technique are frequently and well used in Lu Cuisine. In Bao (quick-fry), foods are deep-fried in very hot oil over high heat and then the oil is poured out and seasonings are added to the food, which is left in the wok. Pa technique, derived from Shandong province, is first to cut the well-cooked ingredient into a particular shape, then stick some powder and fry it into golden, finally add some kind of sauce to sauté it while stirring continuously.

Classic Lu dishes are Stewed Pork Hock(水晶肘子), Braised Colon in Brown Sauce(九转大肠), Dezhou Grilled Chicken, Four Joy Meatballs.

Zhejiang Cuisine

Zhejiang Cuisine, called Zhe Cuisine for short, is originated from South China's Zhejiang Province. It is famous for its mellow, yet not greasy, taste.

It consists of three major styles, namely Hangzhou style, Ningbo style and Shaoxing style. Among them, Hangzhou style is the most notable. It has good taste as well as delicate appearance. It requires expertise in the cooking techniques of quick frying, stir-frying, braising and deep-frying and features clearness, freshness, tenderness, delicateness and purity. Besides seafood and freshwater fish, Hangzhou style exhibits a fondness for bamboo roots. About half the dishes on a Hangzhou menu contain bamboo roots, which add a tender element to the food.

Zhejiang Province, located at the Yangtze River Delta, is the famous "land of milk and honey" in China. Using the rich assortment of local ingredients, Zhe Cuisine has an extensive selection of materials and a precisely matches these materials. Emphasis is placed on the season and variety of main ingredients. The choice of supplementary ingredients and seasonings is aimed to give prominence to the main ingredients, strengthen freshness and fragrance and get rid of the smell of fish and greasiness. Most emphasis is placed on moderation in duration and degree of cooking as well as seasoning.

Classic Zhejiang dishes are Dongpo Pork, Beggar's Chicken, West Lake Fish in Vinegar Gravy, Fish Balls in Clear Soup, Fried Shrimps with Longjing Tea.

Unit 7 Shopping at a Souvenir Shop
在旅游纪念品商店购物

【内容导读】

本单元主要介绍导游在带领游客在旅游纪念品商店购物的过程和环节，包括购物活动的安排、旅游商品推荐、帮助游客讨价还价等环节及其常用用语和句型。

【学习目标】

掌握旅游购物活动安排和旅游商品推荐的技巧及常用句型。

【学习要点】

讨价还价常用用语和句型。

Text

Shopping Experience

Shopping is one of the essential factors of tourism. ① Wherever they go, tourists will buy daily necessities. They will also buy many things needed for a tour, for example, a camera, memory cards, travel bags, tourist maps and drinks. Tourists are always ready to buy special products of local places. For instance, people tend to buy porcelains and silk products in China, clothing, shoes and leather bags in Hong Kong, cosmetics and perfume in U. S. and European countries. The handicrafts stores and souvenir shops are favorite places for tourists to visit. In fact, people always carry some money for shopping during their tour.

Shopping is actually an attraction for tourists. It is especially true for large modern cities such as Hong Kong, London, Paris, New York and Shanghai. Good shopping conditions are sure to attract more tourists. Tourists expect comfortable environment, abundant commodities, dependable quality, reasonable price and good service.

Oral Skills

Procedure and Useful Patterns

Step 1 Tell the guests where they' ll go and explain the reason why they go there.

Useful patterns:

OK, our visit to ... comes to an end. Next, we' ll move to ... shop.

Let' s head for the ... shop. It' s about 20 minutes' drive.

It is well air-conditioned inside the gallery. There are nice Western styled restrooms. We can take a break there, and we can have one of the staff members to give us a brief introduction to Chinese paintings and Chinese calligraphy. So we can get to know something about Chinese culture.

Still, there is a very nice souvenir shop. You can find many special local souvenirs like Chinese paintings, local leaf-vain paintings, embroideries, and silk products. If you are interested, you can buy some for your family members, your relatives and friends.

Well, I remember that on the first day someone asked me if we could find anything special here in Chongqing to keep as souvenir. Still some of the ladies in this group told me that they would like to buy some Chinese dresses for their babies and for themselves. We do have such a place in Chongqing. Now, I just want to know if you would like to pay a visit to the silk shop.

Step 2 Try to arouse the desire of the guests.

What you' ll do is to try to make them interested in the souvenir you want to recommend to them by giving introduction to that which is unique, special, local... Try to introduce the history, production, and features of the souvenir.

Useful patterns:

*I especially would like to recommend you the leaf-vain paintings. It is really a very special local souvenir. It is painted on the leaves of the banyan tree, which is our city tree. The local artists first pick up the banyan tree leaves, put them into a specially-made liquid, and get them dried, then only the vain left and the leaves become as soft as the rice paper*②*. Finally, it is ready for painting. Normally, the artists paint on the leaves flowers, animals like panda bears, landscapes such as the Three Gorges, or city views of Chongqing.*

Step 3 Help the guest bargain.

It is usual for the seller to ask for a high price and give in slowly. The seller makes the starting offer and tries to convince the buyer that his price is reasonable for reasons that the quality is super, or the cost has increased. ③ So it is better for you to help the guest make a counter-offer by pointing out that the starting offer is not reasonable because it is too expensive, or because the quality is not up to standard. You may also suggest some other prices until they agree on the price.

Useful patterns:

Can you give us a discount?

I think that is too dear / expensive. Can you come down a bit?

That's rather more than I / he / she expected. Can you sell it for 150 *yuan?*

How about 150 *yuan?*

That's our rock bottom price. It cannot be further lowered.

150 *yuan, you can't be wrong on that.*

It's too expensive. You know, it is just a work of someone unknown. If you sell it for 150 *yuan, I'll take it.*

Sample 1

Seller: Good afternoon, madam. Can I help you?

Tourist: Yes, please. I'm trying to find some really good Chinese paintings.

Seller: Would you like to see original paintings or reproduction of works by famous artists? ④

Tourist: Please show me original first.

Seller: Here you are. These are original works. They are selling well.

Tourist: How much do you charge for this Chinese painting of flowers and birds?

Seller: You've made a good choice. This kind of painting is extremely popular here. It costs 500 yuan.

Tourist: My God! It's too expensive. You know, it is just a work of someone unknown. If you sell it for 300 yuan, I'll take it.

Seller: But it's really good. (After a moment) OK, I'll sell you. It's really a good buy.

Tourist: Can I pay by credit card?

Seller: Sure.

Sample 2

Seller: Good morning, sir. Are you being served?

Tourist: Good morning. Would you show me some genuine silk ties?

Seller: Certainly, sir. How do you like this one?

Tourist: I'm afraid it's too bright. Please show me some in deep color.

Seller: OK. How about this one? It is of deep color.

Tourist: Oh, it's nice. I like it. How much is it?

Seller: 150 yuan.

Tourist: I'm afraid it's too dear to me. I'd like to buy a cheaper one.

Seller: Maybe this one will suit you. This is just 88 yuan. It's worth every penny of it.

Tourist: Let me have a look.... Ah, I'll take it. Here's 100 yuan.

Seller: Thank you, sir. Take your change, please.

Notes

① Shopping is one of the essential factors of tourism. 购物是旅游的基本要素之一。

② rice paper 宣纸

③ The seller makes the starting offer and tries to convince the buyer that his price is reasonable for reasons that the quality is super, or the cost has increased. 卖方提出开始的报价并试图让买方相信他的价格是合理的,是因为质量超好或者成本涨价了。

④ Would you like to see original paintings or reproduction of works by famous artists? 你想看原作或是知名艺术家作品的复制品?

Words and Expressions

porcelain	*n.* 瓷器
cosmetics	*n.* 化妆品
perfume	*n.* 香水
handicraft	*n.* 手工艺品
souvenir	*n.* 旅游纪念品
dependable	*adj.* 可靠的

reasonable	*adj.* 合理的
calligraphy	*n.* 书法
embroidery	*n.* 绣品;刺绣
arouse	*v.* 引起,唤起;激发
banyan	*n.* 榕树
bargain	*v.* 讨价还价
counter-offer	*n.* 还价,还盘
reproduction	*n.* 复制品
genuine	*adj.* 真正的;纯的
memory card	存储卡
come to an end	结束
leaf-vain paintings	叶脉画

Assignment

Translate the following into English.

(1) 这价格太高了,能降点吗?

(2) 要是 20 元的话,我就要。

(3) 我要向大家特别推荐重庆的火锅底料。

(4) 这件深色的旗袍可能适合你,才 380 元,很便宜。

(5) 我可以用信用卡支付吗?

In-class Practice

Role-play

One of your guests is going to buy some souvenirs. He wants to find something typical of China and at a reasonable price.

Make a conversation according to the above given situation. Try to use the following expressions.

May I help you?

I'm trying to find some small gifts / souvenirs for my parents.

This... is a nice choice.

They can always remind you of your trip to China.

Can you give me a discount?
Can we meet each other half way?
Can you make it... yuan?
This price is quite reasonable.
OK. I' ll take it.

Broaden Your Mind

Silk and Silk Production in China

Silk might be one of the best materials for clothing that has hardly any match in the world. It is light, lustrous, durable, soft to the touch, resistant to heat, and breathing very well, hence it enjoys the fame as the "Queen of Fabrics". And it is an ideal fiber for beautiful Satins, charming brocade, attractive dresses, and comfortable quilts. In the past, only the rich or people from well-to-do families wore silk dresses, which are believed to be commensurate with their social position.

Well-known for its silk production, China is the first silk producer in the world. The silk production started in China about 4,500 years ago. And today we still have three silk production centers in our country: one is in Suzhou and Hangzhou in the lower reaches of the Yangtze River, one is in Sichuan and Chongqing, and one is in Fujian Province in South China.

Silk comes from silkworms. Silkworm breeding is done by the farmers. The farmers breed the worms twice a year: one in Spring, the other in Autumn. They feed the worms with the mulberry leaves (the only food for the worms). And usually it takes about 25 to 30 days for a silkworm to grow old enough to spin a cocoon. When the cocoons are made, they will be sent for reeling. The cocoons be heated in water, then the silk thread is reeled off the cocoon. Do you know how long a silk thread can be got from one cocoon? Yes, it's about 800-1,400 meters long, almost one mile long. Actually a silk thread comes not from one cocoon, but from 6 to 10 cocoons. Then the silk threads are woven into silk. And then varieties of silk products are made, such as silk dresses, silk quilts, silk quilt covers, and embroideries.

A talk about silk is never complete without mentioning the world-famous Silk Road. The Silk Road which was started in the year 139 B. C. was the artery for the two-way flow of goods between China and what we now call the Middle East, Europe and

Africa. At that time China exported huge amount of silk and silk products in exchange for what we needed but didn't produce ourselves, like precious stones, spices, and ivory.

Normally, the Silk Road refers to the route from Xi'An via Xinjiang to the Mediterranean Sea. But in fact, in ancient China we had three Silk Roads. The second is from Sichuan and Chongqing through Yunnan to Southeast Asian countries. The third is on the sea from Quanzhou in Fujian Province through the South China Sea and Indian Ocean to India and Africa.

Unit 8 Seeing Guests off
送团

【内容导读】

本单元介绍送团的过程和程序,送团过程中如何做好告别致辞,包括告别词的结构、内容及常用用语和句型。

【学习目标】

掌握告别致辞的内容组织。

【学习要点】

告别词的结构、内容及常用用语和句型。

Text

Bid Goodbye to the Group

Seeing guests off is meant for the tour guide and the tourist group doing the leaving! Before leaving the hotel, the tour guide will tell the group members to pack their luggage and get them ready. What the tour guide will do is to remind the guests to put metal staffs in checking luggage, and important or valuable things in hand bag (carry-on), remind the guests to clear the safe box in hotel room to make sure nothing is left behind, remind the guests to clear hotel bills①, and tell the guests when to leave for the airport (normally two hours earlier before departure).

At the end of the tour we get to a point where we need to bid goodbye... but it's not always easy to come up with the right words. ②

A good farewell speech can enhance the guests' good impression about the guide, and contribute to the good memories about their travel in your place. Making a farewell speech is also one last chance for the guide to make apologies for inadequate services, and to get suggestions for improvement.

Oral Skills

Process of Seeing Guests off

1. Make sure that no one is missing.

Count the number of guests. You may use:

Is everyone here?

Anyone missing?

2. Remind the guests of their luggage, passport, air ticket, etc..

Is your luggage here?

Are you sure nothing is left behind?

Have a check of your passport, air ticket. Make sure you have them with you.

3. Get on the bus.

You may use:

OK, this is the end of our trip. It's time for the airport.

We have arranged a bus for you to the airport. Let's get on the bus.

4. Explain the check-in process at the airport.

For luggage handling

For security check

For boarding gate

5. Giving Farewell Speech on the bus.

Making a Farewell Speech

1. Beginning.

You may use:

Morning, everyone. Now, we are heading for the airport.

It's about 30 minutes' drive.

Your visit to ... is drawing to a close.

Well, this is the end of your visit to ....

I'd like to say a few words before you leave ... for ....

2. Recall the past days of the tour group (recall what you did).

You may use:

Seven days have passed (elapsed) so quickly.

During the past seven days, you have visited ..., ..., ...

Seven days are rather short and really the surface was only scratched. What the

Chinese people call "looking at the flowers on the horse back".

I have tried to assist you, but as we usually say, you can please some of the people all of the time, some of the other people some of the time, but you cannot please all of the people all of the time.

3. Express thanks.

You may use:

And everyone in this group is very cooperative, friendly, understanding, and punctual. This made our trip very smooth.

As your local guide, it was much appreciated. So I'd like to say thank you. Thanks for your cooperation, your understanding, and your friendliness.

4. Parting, farewell, and give your best wishes.

You may use:

Now it's time for us to say goodbye.

Parting is such sweet sorrow. Happy to meet, sorry to depart, and happy to meet again.

I hope you will come to . . . again.

Goodbye. Have a pleasant journey.

Take care!

Sample Speech 1

Ladies and Gentlemen:

Your visit to China is drawing to a close. I would like to say a few words before you leave this country, though I am not a speech-maker. Seventeen days have passed so quickly and you have visited several cities in our country such as Beijing, Xi'an, Chongqing, particularly the Yangtze River Gorges. Seventeen days' time was rather short and really the surface was only scratched. What the Chinese people call "looking at the flowers on the horse's back". Everybody in this group has been very co-operative, friendly, understanding and punctual. This is what I witnessed and experienced, and as a national guide, it was much appreciated. As you all know that friendship does not go one way, it goes both ways. Of our mixed life, two quests are given control: food for the body and friendship for the soul. I have tried to assist you during your stay in China. You are well aware that one of the fine qualities of true friendship is to understand and to be understood.

The trip of our friends to China is drawing to its end. As we usually say, you can please some of the people all of the time, some of the other people some of the time, but you cannot please all of the people all of the time. However, if you go for a holiday, it doesn't matter whether it is good or bad. If it is bad, you are so pleased to return and appreciate your own home. If it is good, you will be looking forward to going there again. You have not seen anything yet.

Though it is developing fast, tourism in China is a newly-born thing, and the success of tourism can not be achieved by the specialized units alone. Its success depends a great deal on the help and support of units related to this industry. The problems you have met on this trip were known to everyone, and I don't want to enumerate them now, the point is that we should treasure our friendship and experiences.

Now it's time for us to say goodbye. You know, parting is such sweet sorrow. Happy to meet, sorry to depart, and happy to meet again. ③

May the road rise to meet you,
may the wind be always at your back,
may the rain fall softly upon your fields;
May the sun shine warmly upon your face,
and until we meet again.
All the best.

Sample Speech 2

Ladies and Gentlemen:

How time flies! Your visit to Chongqing is drawing to a close. It's time for you to leave for Guangzhou. It's a pity that you cannot stay in Chongqing any longer. Allow me, then, to take this opportunity to say something by way of a farewell.

Your seven-day adoption tour to Chongqing is coming to an end. During the past seven days, we have paid a visit to the orphanage to receive the babies, we have visited the registration office to complete the paper work for the adoption, then we went to the zoo to see the lovely panda bears, and paid a visit to some of the places of interest around Chongqing. Most important of all, we have finished the adoption process very smoothly.

Everyone in this group has kept good time on all occasions, which made things a lot easier for us. You have been very attentive when we had anything to tell you. Also, you have been kind enough to offer me suggestions on how to be a better adoption escort. I wish to thank you for your understanding, your friendliness, your being punctual and for the cooperation and support you have given us in the past seven days.

Seven days ago, we met as strangers. Today, we bid farewell to each other as friends. As goes a Chinese saying, "A good friend from afar brings a distant land closer." I hope you'll take back happy memories of your trip to China, including your visit to Chongqing.

As you have probably observed, Chongqing is developing very fast. Maybe in the future, when and if you come back to Chongqing, the city may have changed beyond recognition. I will continue my job as a local tour guide. I hope to see you again in the future and would like to be your guide again.

Now it's time for us to say goodbye. Hope you enjoy your flight to Guangzhou.

Goodbye.

Bon voyage![4]

Notes

① clear hotel bills 结清酒店账单

② At the end of the tour we get to a point where we need to bid goodbye, but it's not always easy to come up with the right words. 旅行结束时就到了该分别的时候了,然而,要找到合适的话语道别却总是不容易的。

③ Parting is such sweet sorrow. Happy to meet, sorry to depart, and happy to meet again. 离别是如此甜蜜的忧伤。相见时快乐,分离时遗憾,快乐再相见。

④ Bon voyage!(法语)祝一路顺风!一路平安!

Words and Expressions

bid	*v.* 说(问候的话)
farewell	*n.* 告别
inadequate	*adj.* 不足的

clear	*v.* 去除，清除；使清楚；使干净
punctual	*adj.* 守时的，准时的
elapse	*v.*（时间）消逝，过去
enumerate	*v.* 列举，枚举
adoption	*n.* 收养，领养
orphanage	*n.* 孤儿院
smoothly	*adv.* 平稳地，顺利地
attentive	*adj.* 细心的，仔细的；注意的
recognition	*n.* 认识，识别；认可

bid goodbye	说再见；告别
national guide	全陪导游
see sb. off	为某人送行
leave for	出发去（某地）
draw to a close	结束；接近尾声；落幕
by way of	通过（某种方式）

Assignment

Translate the following into English.

（1）我们将于明天早上 8 点离开酒店前往机场，请大家 7 点前准备好行李。

（2）请各位再一次检查一下你的护照和机票，确保带好了。

（3）时间过得真快！你们的中国十日游就要结束了。

（4）请记住一定要清理你房间内的保险箱。

（5）重庆发展得非常快，再过几年，你再到重庆来，可能都认不出来了。

In-class Practice

Role-play

Divide the class into groups (local guide, tourists) to make a conversation according to the situation given below:

Your group's visit to Chongqing is drawing to an end. The guests will leave Chongqing for Guangzhou by flight CA 4135 at 9:00 a.m. tomorrow morning.

The tour guide is telling the guests something about the arrangement.

Broaden Your Mind

Temple of Twin Osmanthus

The Temple of Twin Osmanthus (Shuangguitang) is located 13 km southwest of Liangping County, about 2 and half an hour's ride from the city proper of Chongqing. The founder of the temple Master Poshan planted two osmanthus trees in the temple when the temple was first built in 1661, which are still growing luxuriant. When the two osmanthus trees are in full bloom, one has golden blossoms, and the other has silvery blossoms. Hence the temple was named after the two osmanthus trees as Temple of Twin Osmanthus.

With a history of 350 years, the temple is one of the most important Buddhist temples under state protection in China. And it is well known as the ancestral home of the Chan (or Zen) Sect of Buddhism in the southwest of China.

You know, Buddhism was from ancient India. It has many different schools, like the Esoteric Buddhism, Huayan Buddhism, Tiantai Buddhism, Chan Buddhism, and even Lamaism. But only the Huayan, Tiantai, and Chan were originally and independently developed in China, of the three, the Chan Sect is most popular among Chinese people (since it was well combined with traditional Chinese moral concept like being loyal, being obedience to parents, retribution for sin etc.). The word "Chan" comes from Sanskrit word Zen, which means the course of practicing Buddhism by sitting still and being in deep meditation so that enlightenment can be attained.

Covering an area of 7 hectares, the temple is constructed in the form of a rectangular courtyard which is 360 meters long from east to west, and 256 meters wide from south to north, consisting of 7 hall buildings and 328 rooms. The whole complex is a wooden and stone structure well furnished for Buddhist activities. The layout of the temple was rationally and exquisitely designed. The 7 hall buildings are arranged standing one after another on the axis in the middle of the courtyard from the front to the back, and the 328 rooms are on its two sides. All the buildings and rooms in the temple are connected with long corridors, making it possible and convenient for the monks and worshippers walk around and get to any building even in rainy days.

The 7 hall buildings are:

The Big Entrance Hall (大山门), also called the Hall of Sage Guan(关圣殿), it is for worshipping Sage Guan Yu, who was a famous general during the Three Kingdoms Period (the third century). Since Guan Yu was very famous for being brave and loyal to his sworn brother Liu Bei, the king of Shu Kingdom, and he has become the symbol of bravery and loyalty in Chinese culture, so he was worshipped as the guardian of Buddha(护法神) by Buddhist believers.

The Maitreya Hall (弥勒殿) is for worshipping Maitreya (弥勒). Maitreya has a very big belly, and he is always laughing as if he is always very happy. Chinese people say his big belly can tolerate anything intolerable and his smiling shows that he is laughing at the funny things about people and those laughable people. He is believed to be Buddha of Future(来世佛).

The Mahavira Hall (大雄宝殿), also called the Grand Hall, it is for worshipping Buddha Sakyamuni (释迦牟尼), the founder of Buddhism, Buddha of Present(现世佛). The Mahavira Hall is the main hall and the most imposing building in the temple. It is a 3-storey palatial building with saddle roofs and flying eaves(歇山重檐式建筑), supported by 52 stone pillars. Each pillar is about 9 meters tall, 0.7 meter in diameter, and 10 tons in weight.

The Hall of Disciplines(文殊殿) is for worshipping Manjusri(文殊菩萨), Bodhisattva of wisdom. It was the first building in this temple. The hall is a two-storey wooden structure with saddle roofs and without a single nail.

The Poshan Pagoda (破山塔) is a hexagon-shaped stone pagoda which is about 7 meters tall and 4 meters in diameter. It was for keeping relics or ashes of Master Poshan, the founder and the first abbot of the temple. According to Buddhism, only the eminent monks could be cremated and be buried in a pagoda after their death.

The Hall of Great Mercy (大悲殿) is for worshipping Bodhisattva Guanyin, Goddess of Mercy, also Mother God in Esoteric Buddhism.

The Hall of Relics(舍利殿), known as the Depositary of Buddhist Sutra(藏经楼), is for keeping relics or ashes of Buddha, and also for keeping Buddhist scriptures.

Besides the 7 halls, there is the Hall of Arhats(罗汉堂), which was built in recent years. Inside the hall there are 500 painted clay sculptures of arhats.

Arhat is a Sanskrit word, referring to the 500 Buddha's followers on the third level of position, who are believed to be detached from any worry or any trouble, and no longer goes into retribution. According to Buddhist doctrines, there are three final results of practicing Buddhism: on the very top is Buddha, next are 8 Bodhisattvas, and the third level are arhats.

The Temple of Twin Osmanthus (Shuangguitang) also features numerous stone steles, wooden carvings, painted clay sculptures, Chinese paintings and calligraphies, all of which are imbued with a strong religious feeling.

Part Ⅱ Outbound Tour Leader 出境领队

Unit 9 Taking an International Flight
乘坐国际航班

【内容导读】

本单元介绍国际旅行中乘机的程序，包括办理登机手续、行李托运、超重行李处理、过境与转机，以及飞行过程中要求机上服务的常用用语及句型。

【学习目标】

熟悉乘坐国际航班的程序和一般规则，掌握常用用语及句型。

【学习要点】

转机与要求机上服务的常用用语及句型。

Text

International Travel

When going on an international flight, it's important to get to the airport early, to drink enough water when flying and to dress comfortably. When traveling internationally, it's important to take a copy of a passport and to make sure that the passport expires at least six months after the departure date.①

Please note that airport check-in begins 2 hours and closes 40 minutes before departure. Don't forget that at the airport you are obliged to pass Security Control and, if you are taking an international flight, Customs and Passport Control, too. Please be on time. The boarding gate closes 20 minutes before departure.

Oral Skills

Ⅰ. Check-in at the Airport

Procedure and Useful Patterns

Step 1 Finding check-in counter.

Is this the counter for ... to ...?

Could you tell me where I should check in for ... to ...?

Excuse me. Should I check in here for taking flight... to ...?

Excuse me. Where do we check in our luggage?

Please go to the counter beside the information desk.

Please go to the next counter for group check-in.

Down to the far end of the lounge and you'll find the counter for flights to ....

Step 2　Asking for seat arrangement.

Can I have a seat in the back of the plane?

We are from the same tour group. Can we have ... window seats and ... aisle seats?

We are a group of 30 *people. Can we have our seats close to each other?*

Er, let me see. It is quite full now. I can hardly give you 30 *seats together. But I'll try to make it for you.*

Step 3　Dealing with overweight luggage.

What's the luggage allowance[②]*, please?*

Could you explain the free baggage allowance to me?

For checking luggage, it's 30*kg free luggage allowance for first class and* 20*kg for economy class.*

Your free luggage allowance is not more than 23*kg each.*

The allowance for the carry-on baggage is 5*kg.*

They are not overweight, are they?

They are 5*kg over.*

Your luggage is 3*kg overweight.*

Probably you could pick something out of your luggage and take them with you / put them in your carry-on luggage.

Sample Dialogue

Tour Leader: Excuse me. Is this the counter for Flight QR881 to Doha?

Airport Clerk: Yes, sir. What can I do for you?

Tour Leader: We are a tour group of 20 people. We'd like to check in now.

Airport Clerk: I'm sorry. Please go to Counter 4 for group check-in.

Tour Leader: OK. Thank you. (Turn to Counter 4) Hello, should we check in here for flight to Doha?

Airport Clerk: Yes, sir. May I have your passports, please?

Tour Leader: Sure, here are 20 passports. We are from the same tour group. Can we have our seats close to each other?

Airport Clerk: Let me see. I can hardly give you 20 seats together, but I'll try to make it for you.

Tour Leader: Thank you very much.

Airport Clerk: How many pieces of luggage do you want to check in?

Tour Leader: We got 20 suitcases.

Airport Clerk: Please put them on the scale one by one.

Tour Leader: OK.

Airport Clerk: I'm sorry, sir. This one is overweight.

Tour Leader: Really? What's the luggage allowance, please?

Airport Clerk: It's not more than 23kg each. And this suitcase is 3kg over.

Tour Leader: That's too bad.

Airport Clerk: Probably you could pick something out and take them with you. You know, you can have 5kg of carry-on baggage.

Tour Leader: That's a good idea.

Airport Clerk: Sir, I have arranged your seats as close to each other as possible. Here are your passports, boarding passes and your luggage claim tags. Enjoy your flight.

Tour Leader: Thank you for your help.

Airport Clerk: My pleasure.

Ⅱ. Transit and Transfer

Procedure and Useful Patterns

Step 1 Check in for transfer.

Where should I take my connecting flight?

Can I make a connecting flight[3] *here to ...?*

We are to transfer to Flight ... to .... We'd like to check in now.

Excuse me. We'll have to transfer here and continue our journey to ..., what should we do?

We have to change our flight to .... Shall we go to the Transfer Counter and recheck in?

Shall we get a new boarding pass?

Step 2 Finding boarding gate.

Will passengers for Flight... to ... please go to Gate 11.

Could you tell me the way to the boarding gate?

We have a connecting flight on ... to .... Where should we board the plane?

Just take the escalator down to the next floor, get on the passenger conveyer to the departure lounge, and you can easily find the boarding gate 23.

Sample Dialogue

Tour Leader: Excuse me.

Airport Clerk: Yes. May I help you?

Tour Leader: We'll have to transfer here and continue our journey to London, what should we do?

Airport Clerk: You would have to go to the Transfer Counter and recheck in.

Tour Leader: Shall we get a new boarding pass?

Airport Clerk: Yes, you will.

Tour Leader: But how can we get to the Transfer Counter?

Airport Clerk: Just go straight and then turn left. You can see the sign.

Tour Leader: I see. Thank you for your help.

(At the Transfer Counter)

Airport Clerk: Good evening, sir. May I help you?

Tour Leader: Yes, we are a tour group of ten and we are to transfer to Flight QR880 to London. We'd like to check in now.

Airport Clerk: Your passports and tickets, please.

Tour Leader: Certainly, here you are. Can we have four window seats and six aisle seats?

Airport Clerk: OK. No problem. Do you have any luggage to check in?

Tour Leader: No.

Airport Clerk: A moment please. Alright, here are your air tickets, passports and boarding passes. You will board from Gate 23, and the boarding time is 1:00 a. m.

Tour Leader: How can we find Gate 23 from here?

Airport Clerk: Just take the escalator down to the next floor, get on the passenger conveyer[4] to the departure lounge, and you can easily find the boarding gate 23.

Tour Leader: Thank you.

Airport Clerk: Welcome.

Ⅲ. On the Plane

Procedure and Useful Patterns

Step 1 Ordering drinks and meals.

Do you need anything to drink, sir?

What kind of drinks do you like?

We have coffee, tea, juice, coke, mineral water and beer, which one do you prefer?

Pineapple juice is not available, how about tomato juice?

Excuse me, miss. Could you get us something to drink, please?

Orange juice for the lady by the window and coffee for me, please.

Please give him some hot tea.

They just want some mineral water.

Could you please get the gentleman some more beer?

What would you like, rice or noodles?

We have rice with chicken and noodles with beef. Which one do you prefer?

I'll order for them. Rice with chicken for the two young ladies, and noodles with beef for the old lady and the three gentlemen. Thank you.

Just give her chicken and juice, and I'd like beef, please.

Could you please give her vegetarian dish?

Step 2 Asking for in-flight services.

Excuse me, miss. I need a headset.

Miss, can I have a blanket and pillow, please?

Would you please give the old lady a blanket? She feels a little bit cold.

Excuse me, miss. One of our group members is not feeling well. Can I bother you for a cup of hot water, please? / Would you please bring a cup of hot water for her?

Sample Dialogue

Tour Leader: Excuse me, miss. One of our group members is not feeling well. Can I bother you for a cup of hot water, please?

Air Hostess: Certainly, sir. Just a moment please. Sir, here's the hot water. Is she all right?

Tour Leader: She feels a little bit cold. Would you please give her a blanket?

Air Hostess: Sure. I'll be back with the blanket in a minute.

Tour Leader: Thank you so much.

(A moment later)

Air Hostess: Ladies and gentlemen, we'll be serving you meal. We have rice with chicken and noodles with beef. Which one do you prefer, sir? And how about you, madam?

Tour Leader: Well, I'll order for them. Rice with chicken for the two young ladies, and noodles with beef for the old lady and the three gentlemen. Thank you.

Air Hostess: All right, two rice with chicken , and four noodles with beef . Here you are.

Tour Leader: Could you please give vegetarian dish to the old lady over there?

Air Hostess: Sure. But what would you like?

Tour Leader: I prefer chicken rice.

Air Hostess: And what kind of drinks do they prefer, please?

Tour Leader: (After a while) Mineral water for the old lady over there, the two young ladies want some orange juice, and just give the three gentlemen beer, and coffee for me, please.

Air Hostess: OK. Anything else?

Tour Leader: Not at the moment.[⑤] Thank you.

Air Hostess: You are welcome.

Notes

① ... make sure that the passport expires at least six months after the departure date. ……要确保护照的有效期为六个月。

② luggage allowance 允许免费托运的行李重量

③ connecting flight 驳接航班,转接航班

④ passenger conveyer 乘客传送带;电动步行带

⑤ Not at the moment. 暂时没有了。

Words and Expressions

overweight	*adj.* 超重的
carry-on	*n.* 随身行李
scale	*n.* 秤
transit	*v.* 过境
transfer	*v.* 转机;转乘
escalator	*n.* 电动扶梯
conveyer	*n.* 传送带
vegetarian	*adj.* 素食的
headset	*n.* 耳机
blanket	*n.* 毯子
pillow	*n.* 枕头

Doha	多哈(卡塔尔首都)
be obliged to do ...	有义务做…;不得不做…
Security Control	安检
check in	办理登机手续
window seat	靠窗的座位
aisle seat	靠过道的座位
checking luggage	需要托运的行李
luggage claim tag	行李标签
boarding pass	登机牌
boarding gate	登机口
rice with chicken	鸡肉米饭
noodles with beef	牛肉面

Assignment

Translate the following into English.

(1) 你的行李超重了5公斤。

(2) 请乘坐飞往东京的NH588航班的旅客到7号登机口登机。

(3) 小姐,可以给我一张毛毯吗?

(4) 恐怕他是晕机了,请给他倒杯开水好吗?

(5) 请问,我可以在这里转机到洛杉矶吗?

In-class Practice

Role-play

Divide the class into groups (tour leader, airport clerk) to make a conversation according to the situation given below:

When you are checking in for transfer, one of your guest's luggage is 2kg over, try to deal with it.

Discussion

When you are waiting for the flight in the airport waiting hall, the airport broadcast announced that the flight your group is going to take was cancelled. As a tour leader, how will you do?

Broaden Your Mind

Traveling in Europe

If you are a non-EU national wishing to visit or travel within the E. U., you will need a passport valid for at least 3 months after the date you intend to leave the E. U. country you are visiting, which was issued within the previous 10 years, and possibly a visa. Apply for a visa from the consulate or embassy of the country you are visiting. If your visa is from a "Schengen area" country, it automatically allows you to travel to the other Schengen countries as well. If you have a valid residence permit from one of those Schengen countries, it is equivalent to a visa. You may need a national visa to visit non-Schengen countries.

Border officials in E. U. countries may ask for other supporting documents such as an invitation letter, proof of lodging, return or round-trip ticket. For the precise requirements contact the local consular services of the E. U. country in question.

There are a number of countries whose nationals do not need a visa to visit the E. U. for three months or less. The list of countries whose nationals require visas to travel to the United Kingdom or Ireland differs slightly from other E. U. countries.

Europe has a high season in summer and another in winter. Crowding is the main difficulty in the warmest months of June, July and particularly August. In some countries, such as France and Italy, many shops and restaurants close in August while locals take their own holidays, meaning that some cities can feel rather dead.

Global warming has meant a later start to the skiing season; often, decent snowfalls aren't recorded until January (or even February). December is always busy in locations such as Paris, Prague and any Austrian or German city with a quaint Christmas market. Easter is another busy time.

You can find bargains by visiting traditionally "summer" destinations such as Greece in winter, but be aware that public transport might be less frequent. In some northern locations such as Scotland and Scandinavia, it might not run at all as heavy snow and ice mean services are seasonal.

For all the above reasons, by far the best months to travel in Europe are May, June and September.

Unit 10 Immigration and Emigration
办理出入境手续

【内容导读】

本单元介绍出境旅游团队出入境的程序、出入境手续办理,包括出入境卡填写、通关等环节。

【学习目标】

熟悉出入境程序,熟练掌握出入境手续办理规则,以及常用用语和句型。

【学习要点】

出入境卡的填写。

Text

Emigration and Immigration

Emigration is the act of leaving one's native country with the intent to settle elsewhere. Conversely, immigration describes the movement of persons into a country to which they are not native.

When travelling internationally, make sure you have a valid passport and all other documentation required to satisfy the entry requirements of all the countries you will be visiting including transit countries and for returning home. Depending on your passport nationality and destination, additional requirements may include a minimum period of passport validity, visas, the need for a return or onward ticket, a returning resident visa, and sufficient funds for your stay.

If your travel documentation is incomplete or inadequate you will not be permitted to board your flight. To avoid any inconvenience and possible additional costs, please check that you meet the requirements for your destination(s) as well as any countries you will pass through in transit.

Vaccinations and other medical precautions are recommended and in some cases required for travel to some countries, and are easily obtained through your doctor. Have them well before you leave to allow time for them to become effective and to recover from any possible side effects. ①

Oral Skills

Ⅰ. Immigration Formalities

Procedure and Useful Patterns

Step 1 Filling out entry card②.

May I have some entry cards and customs declarations?

Step 2 Going through the immigration.

May I have your passport and arrival card, please?

I' m the leader of a tour group. We have a group visa.

How long will you be staying in ... ?

You are cleared. ③

Please let your passengers keep their arrival cards in their passports, and go through one by one according to the order of the name list.

Sample Dialogue

(A = Immigration Officer; B = Tour Leader)

A: Good afternoon, sir. May I have your passport and arrival card, please?

B: Good afternoon. I' m the leader of a tour group. We have a group visa.

A: Please show it to me.

B: Certainly, sir. Here you are.

A: How long will your group be staying in U. K. ?

B: 7 days. We' ll be leaving on July 11.

A: Sir, why is this passenger' s date of birth different from that in her passport?

B: Let me see. Oh, I' m sorry. I had made a mistake when I filled in the visa form. I' ll correct it right now.

A: Please let your passengers keep their arrival cards in their passports, and go through one by one according to the order of the name list.

B: All right. Can I be the last one to pass, sir?

A: Sure, you can.

(a moment later)

A: OK. I think you are cleared. Thank you for your cooperation.

B: Thank you.

Ⅱ. Customs Clearance

Procedure and Useful Patterns

Step 1 Customs declaration.

Please show your customs declaration form, sir.

May I have your declaration form?

Do you have anything to declare? / Anything to declare?

Step 2 Going through customs.

Will you open your suitcase, please?

You'll have to pay duty on that.

You may go through now.

You are passed. /You are cleared.

Sample Dialogue

(A = Customs Inspector; B = Tourist)

A: Anything to declare?

B: I suppose no.

A: Will you open your suitcase, please?

B: Certainly, sir.

A: Do you have any liquor or cigarettes?

B: Yes, I have a carton of cigarettes and two bottles of Chinese dry wine Maotai as gifts for my friend. That's duty-free, isn't it?

A: I'm afraid not. You can bring in only one carton of cigarettes and one bottle of liquor duty-free. You'll have to pay duty on that. You need to fill in this declaration form and take it to that official at the exit.

B: OK. I'll do that.

A: What are these?

B: These are my personal belongs. Some clothes, a shaving kit, and a pack of green tea.

A: Is this a new camera?

B: No, it's an old one. It's for my own use.

A: All right. You may go through now.

Notes

① Have them well before you leave to allow time for them to become effective and to recover from any possible side effects. 在出发之前把这些文件准备好,确保这些文件在有效期内,并能从任何不良反应中恢复过来。

② entry card 入境卡(有的国家称为 arrival card 或 landing card)

③ You are cleared. 你没问题了(你已获准通过)。

Words and Expressions

emigration	*n.* 出境
immigration	*n.* 入境
valid	*adj.* 有效的
validity	*n.* 有效期
vaccination	*n.* 免疫
formality	*n.* 手续
customs	*n.* 海关
declare	*v.* 申报
duty	*n.* 税
side effect	副作用
customs declaration	海关申报;报关
group visa	团队签证
go through	通过
a carton of	一条
shaving kit	刮胡刀

Assignment

Translate the following into English.

(1) 我随团旅行。我是该团的领队。

(2) 我能核对一下你的护照吗?

(3) 你的行李已经放行。

（4）你得为你带的两瓶酒付关税。
（5）请将入境卡夹在护照里，然后依次通过。

In-class Practice

Fill out the arrival card according to the information below.

Family name______________ **Given or first names**______________

Sex □ **M** □ **F**

Town and Country of birth______________________________

Nationality______________ **Occupation**______________

Contact address in the UK (in full)

____

Passport number____________ **Place of Issue**______________

Length of stay in the UK______________________________

Port of last departure______________________________

Arrival flight / train number / ship name____________________

Signature

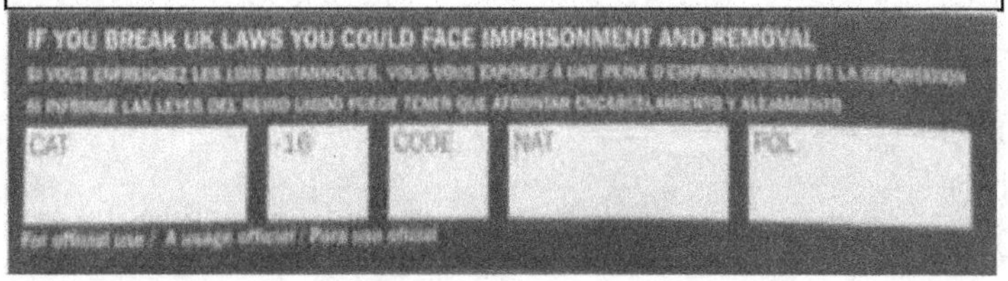

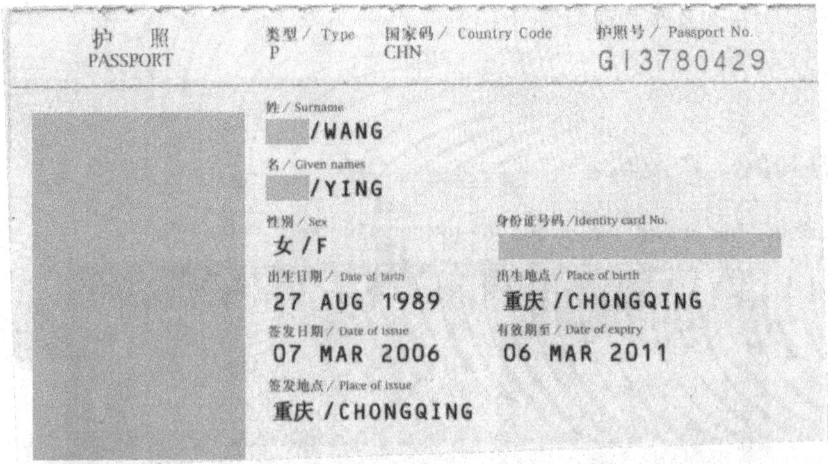

AIRLINE PNR:4O8CPP	1E PNR:HM1DRY
NAME:WANG YING	ETKT NBR:074-4720426181
ID NUMBER:	CONJ NBR:
ISSUING AIRLINE:KLM ROYAL DUTCH AIRLINES	DATE OF ISSUE:10OCT14
ISSUING AGENT:	IATA CODE:08309836

ORIGIN/DES	FLIGHT	CLASS	DATE	TIME	PERIOD	STATUS	ALLOW
CHENGDU—AMS	KL892	V	29NOV	1530	29NOV4/29NOV4	OK	1PC
AMS —NEWCASTLE	KL971	L	29NOV	2150	29NOV4/29NOV4	OK	1PC
NEWCASTLE—AMS	KL964	L	07DEC	1725	07DEC4/07DEC4	OK	1PC
AMS—CHENGDU	KL891	V	07DEC	2055	07DEC4/07DEC4	OK	1PC

U. K. address
11 Kipling Walk
Gateshead
NE8 3NT

Broaden Your Mind

Travel Documents

When traveling internationally, it is imperative that you research the passport and visa requirements of your destination countries prior to departure. Depending on your country of origin and arrival, a passport and visa may be required to enter the country, and understanding the difference between and purpose of each will make the amount of time spent in the customs line as minimal as possible.

A travel document is an identity document issued by a government or international treaty organization to facilitate the movement of individuals or small groups of persons across international boundaries. Travel documents usually assure other governments that the bearer may return to the issuing country, and are often issued in booklet form to allow other governments to place visas as well as entry and exit stamps into them. The most common travel document is a passport, which usually gives the bearer more privileges like visa-free access to certain countries.

Passport

A passport is a universally accepted international document that is sufficient for crossing the border and provides a person's identity and nationality. It is issued by the traveler's country of origin and provides proof of citizenship.

Visa

A visa is a document granting permission for entry into a country to fulfill a specific purpose. A visa is granted by the country the traveler is visiting and is typically stamped into the traveler's passport.

Before entering a foreign country, travelers must usually obtain a visa. A visa is an endorsement made in a passport, which allows the passport holder to enter the country issuing the visa.

Arrival Card

An arrival card, also be known as an incoming passenger card, landing card, entry card or disembarkation card, is a legal document used by immigration authorities to provide passenger identification and a record of a person's entry into certain countries. It also provides information on health and character requirements for non-citizens entering a particular country. Some countries such as the United States and Singapore attach the card to a departure card where the latter is retained in the alien's passport until his eventual departure. The arrival card can also be combined with items found in a customs declaration card which some countries require incoming passengers to fill out separately.

Departure Card

A departure card, also known as an outgoing passenger card or embarkation card, is a legal document used by immigration authorities to provide passenger identification and an effective record of a person's departure from certain countries.

Travelers are generally required to sign, date, and declare the information is true, correct, and complete.

Passengers on international flights are often required to complete the cards and are often required to present the cards and their passports at immigration checkpoints. Some countries, most notably those in the Schengen Zone don't require aliens to complete this card.

The information requested varies by country. Typically the information requested on the arrival card or departure card includes:

- Full name;
- Nationality;
- Date of Birth;
- Passport number, place of issuance and expiry date;
- Flight number or name of aircraft, ship or vehicle;
- Purpose of trip: vacation, education/study, visiting relatives/families, business, diplomatic;
- Duration of stay;
- Destination (next stop of disembarkation);
- Address in country.

Unit 11 Tax Refund
退税

【内容导读】

本单元介绍境外购物退税相关知识，包括退税政策及退税手续办理、流程等内容。

【学习目标】

了解境外主要国家购物退税政策，熟悉退税手续办理与常用用语及句型。

【学习要点】

退税单的填写。

Text

Sales Tax Refunds for Visitors

Some countries provide the sales tax refund policies. Why countries allow sales tax refunds for visitors? The reason is simple—visitor attraction. Countries want you to spend, spend and spend when you are visiting, so offering a tax refund works the same way as someone putting a sign that says "Big Discount". ① Most countries have different procedures of applying for tax refunds as well as which part of the sales tax can be refunded. However, the general procedure consists of:

Filling out some type of form;

Bringing your passport;

Proof that you are a visitor—some form of boarding pass or itinerary etc.

As a tour leader, it is your responsibility to help the visitors in your group to get tax refunds back.

Oral Skills

Refund at a Shop

Procedure and Useful Patterns

Step 1　Inquiring about tax exemption[②].

Can I get a refund for this?

Can we get a tax refund for... we just bought?

Please show me how to claim the tax refund.

Step 2　Filling out tax refund form.

Can I have a tax refund form, please?

Just fill in your name, passport number, nationality and home address.

Where can we get our tax refund?

You can draw it back at the customs with this refund form.

Take this form, together with your passport, boarding pass, and the item you bought to the Customs Certification at the airport for stamping[③].

Then you can get your tax refund with the stamped refund form at the Cash Refund at the Emigration.

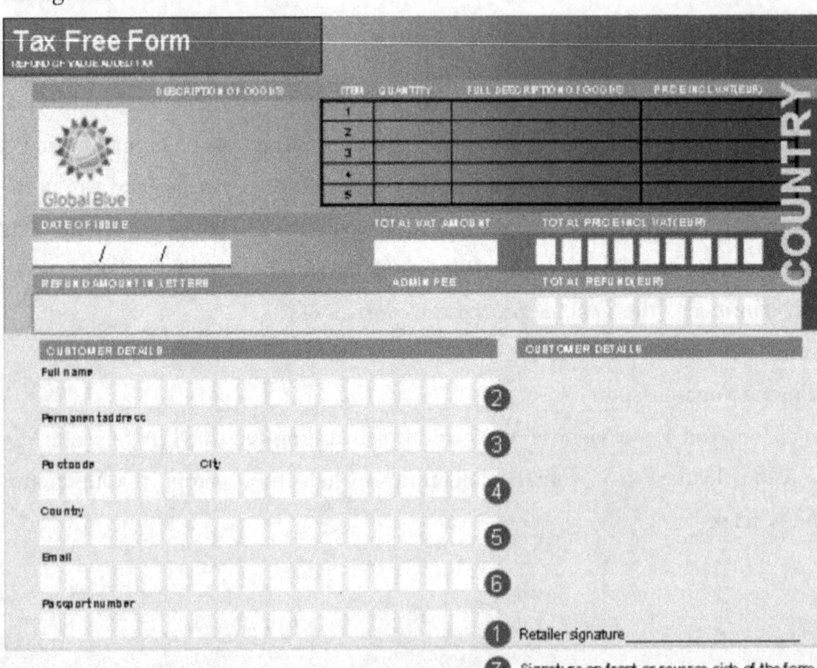

White Tax Free Form

CUSTOMER DETAILS

Passport / ID No. :

1

Name:

2

Permanent home address:

3

ZIP / City:

4

Country:

5

Email address:

6

DECLARATION:

I confirm the Customer Declaration and consent to the processing of my personal data for refund of VAT as set out in the Privacy Notice overleaf or in a separate document hereby submitted to me.

I consent to the processing of my personal data for marketing purposes.

CUSTOMER SIGNATURE: 7 ________________

Step 3　Getting tax refund back.

Is this the place where I can draw back the tax paid for... I bought in...?

May I get my tax refund here?

How would you like to get it, get it in cash or send it to your credit account?

Sample Dialogue

(A = Tour Leader; B = Shop Assistant; C = Custom Official; D = Cash Refund Clerk)

A: Excuse me, miss. We are tourists from China. Can we get a tax refund for the camera we bought?

B: Of course, sir. May I see your passport?

A: Here you are.

B: All right, sir. I'll give you each a tax refund form. You just fill in your name, passport number, nationality, home address and your credit card account on the form. Don't forget to put your signature on the form.

A: I see. How much money can we get back?

B: Well, the tax is about 16%. And you've paid 628 Euros④ for the camera, so you'll get a refund of 100.5 Euros.

A: After filling out the form, what should we do?

B: Put the refund form and the receipt into this envelope. When you are leaving the European Union countries, remember to put it into the Tax Refund Mail Box at any international airport. Your refund will be transferred into your credit card account.

A: Do we have any other options?

B: You may also draw it back at the customs when you are leaving. Take this form, together with your passport, boarding pass, and the item you bought to the Customs Certification at the airport for stamping. Then you can get your tax refund with the stamped refund form at the Cash Refund at the Emigration, either in cash or send it to your credit account.

A: Thank you for your explanation.

B: My pleasure.

...

A: Excuse me, sir. Is this the place where we can draw back our tax refund?

C: Yes, sir. Show me your tax refund form, passport, boarding pass, and the item you bought, please.

A: Here you are.

C: (After stamping the tax refund form) All right, sir. Please go to the Cash Refund Counter at the Emigration to get your tax refund.

A: Thank you.

...

A: Good morning, miss. I'd like to get my tax refund.

D: Certainly, sir. May I have your stamped tax refund form, passport, boarding pass, please?

A: Here you are.

D: How would you like to have it, in cash or sent it to your credit account?

A：Cash, please.

D：All right. Here are your passport, boarding pass and 100.5 Euros tax refund.

A：Thank you very much.

Notes

① . . . so offering a tax refund works the same way as someone putting a sign that says "Big Discount". ……提供退税与某人手举写有"大减价"的牌子作用一样。

② tax exemption 免税;不用付税

③ for stamping 去盖章

④ Euro (货币单位)欧元

Words and Expressions

refund	*n.* & *v.* 退款;资金偿还
procedure	*n.* 步骤;程序
claim	*v.* 索取;领取
stamp	*v.* 盖章;贴标记于…
proof	*v.* 证明
consent (to)	*v.* 同意;赞同
overleaf	*adv.* 在本页背面
submit	*v.* 提交;呈送
receipt	*n.* 发票;收据
transfer	*v.* 转移;转

tax refund	退税
tax refund form	退税表;退税单
work the same way as. . .	跟…相同;与…起同样的作用
VAT (Value Added Tax)	增值税

Assignment

Translate the following into English.

(1) 请问,我刚刚买的这双鞋可以退税吗? 退税率是多少?

(2) 请告诉我该如何申请退税。
(3) 我可以要求现金退税吗?
(4) 你的退税款将转入你的信用卡账户。
(5) 如果我不想现金退税,我还有其他选择吗?

In-class Practice

Role-play

Divide the class into groups (tour leader, salesperson) to make a conversation according to the situation given below:

You want to know if you can get a tax refund for the commodities you are going to buy, the rate for the tax refund, the place and the procedure for claiming tax refund.

Broaden Your Mind

Tax-free Shopping

Tax-free shopping refers to the opportunity for customers to purchase goods or services without paying any tax normally collected at retail, such as sales tax, Goods and Services Tax, value added tax, or consumption tax.

Tax-free shopping (TFS) allows shoppers to reclaim the VAT (Value-Added Tax)/GST (Goods and Services Tax) they have paid on their shopping in foreign countries. Promoting the tax rebate and making it easier for tourists to claim it back, has helped to attract travellers to many countries. Fifty-two of the 130 countries that levy VAT/GST allow foreign visitors to have their taxes reimbursed. TFS is subject to national regulations, such as minimum spend and restrictions on the types of products on which it can be claimed. Refunds can only be claimed on goods which are exported. However, buying goods tax free whilst on holiday does not mean travellers are exempt from paying applicable taxes on their purchases when they get home.

Approximately 52,000 people benefit each day from tax free shopping around the world. Tax-free shopping services are available from more than 320,000 stores in 52 countries worldwide.

Tax-free shopping is available in the following countries: Argentina, Australia, Austria, Belgium, Croatia, Cyprus, Czech Republic, Denmark, Estonia, Finland,

France, Germany, Greece, Hungary, Iceland, Indonesia, Ireland, Israel, Italy, Japan, Korea, Latvia, Lebanon, Liechtenstein, Lithuania, Luxembourg, Malaysia, Mexico, Morocco, the Netherlands, Norway, Poland, Portugal, Serbia, Singapore, Slovenia, Slovakia, Spain, South Africa, Sweden, Switzerland, Thailand, Turkey, the United States, the United Kingdom and Vietnam.

Tax refund is provided by GB Tax Free, VP Tax Free, Global Blue, Premier Tax Free, Eurorefund, vatfree. com, FEXCO Tax Free, Yvesam Tax Refund Services, and Euro Free Shopping.

The refunded amount corresponds to the VAT or GST paid and in which country the traveller buys goods. VAT/GST is a tax added to the cost of a product, calculated as a percentage of the products retail price. Often in Europe the ticket price includes VAT, this is less often the case in the U. S. As an example, if the VAT rate on a product is 20% and the ticket price is displayed as 100, including VAT, the VAT will be 16.67 (83.5 + 20% VAT = 100.). A handling fee may be charged by the service provider.

All travellers living in a country outside the E. U. , are privileged to shop tax-free at shops outside E. U. airports. The traveller pays the VAT over goods in the shop, and can request for a refund when exporting the goods. General restrictions are that a traveller must have residency in a non-E. U. country, has a maximum stay of 6 months when visiting the E. U. , purchases are made up to three months prior to export, only goods meant for personal use are eligible for the refund. Travellers need to save purchase receipts and visit Customs before leaving the E. U. to get an export validation stamp. Receipts can then be sent back to the retailers for a refund request.

Some jurisdictions in the United States allow the refund of sales tax to foreign tourists upon exiting the country, e. g. Texas.

Unit 12 Handling Emergencies
紧急情况处理

【内容导读】

本单元介绍境外旅行中紧急情况的处理，包括游客走失、游客生病、护照遗失、交通事故等。

【学习目标】

熟练掌握游客走失、游客生病、护照遗失、交通事故等紧急情况的处理程序和技巧，以及常用用语和句型。

【学习要点】

有关游客病情描述、交通事故描述常用用语和句型。

Text

Emergencies during travelling abroad are commonplace for foreign visitors and can occasionally have serious consequences. Therefore, the tour leader must get familiar with some possible emergencies, such as outbreak of infectious disease, food poisoning, terrorist attack, military coup, and natural disasters like earthquake, mud-rock flow, landslide, flood, tsunami, typhoon, and snow. Sometimes the tourist may leave their personal belongings behind, get their passports lost, or tourists getting sick, tourists getting lost, or being in a traffic accident when on a sightseeing tour. The tour leader must learn effective ways to deal with these emergencies and useful expressions on handling emergencies. You should also make every effort to help the tourists. This will help to keep the tour going smoothly.

When an emergency occurs, the first thing for a tour leader to do is to give an alarm and organize rescue. You should promptly call the local police, the local rescue organization as well as the travel agency in the host country. You should also organize on-site first aid to the wounded tourists, maintain order and comfort other panic-stricken tourists.

Then, the next thing you will do is to report to your domestic tour organizing travel agency. If it is a serious accident, you need to report to Chinese embassy or consulate for help. You should also collect evidences such as medical certificate, police evidence and materials for the needs of subsequent claims and dispute resolution.

Oral Skills

Ⅰ. Tourist Lost

Procedure and Useful Patterns

Step 1 Tell the local guide that sb. is missing.

Someone is missing, I'm afraid.

The old lady sitting behind me is not here.

I haven't seen Mr. Liu. I'm afraid he is getting lost.

Step 2 Looking for missing tourist.

We are looking for a Chinese old man. Did you see him here?

What does she look like?

He is tall/short and thin/fat, wearing a white shirt and blue trousers.

Sample Dialogue

(A = John, Local Guide; B = Tour Leader; C = Park Staff)

A: Is everybody on the bus?

B: Let me see. Er, John, I haven't seen Mr. Liu. I'm afraid he is getting lost. We must find him.

A: Probably he is left behind in the park. Can you make a phone call to see if we can contact him?

B: I'm sorry. He doesn't have a cell phone[①] with him.

A: Then we'll have to go to find him. Well, there are three entrances in the park. I'll go to that side entrance. Would you please go to the other side entrance?

B: All right. (To the park staff at the side entrance) Excuse me, sir. I'm looking for a Chinese old man. Did you see him here?

C: What does he look like?

B: He is tall and thin, wearing a white shirt and blue trousers.

C: Does he have a folding fan in his hand?

B: Yes, and with a black pack on his back.

C: That's him. He has been here about five minutes ago.

B: Where did he go?

C: I saw him taking the left path to the back entrance.

B: Thank you.

C: Welcome.

...

B: John, I've got him. He failed to catch up with the group and turned the wrong way to the back entrance.

A: Thank god. It's my fault. I haven't taken care of him. I do apologize for it.

B: That's all right. You are always so considerate.

Ⅱ. Tourist Got Sick

Procedure and Useful Patterns

Step 1 Send the sick tourist to a hospital.

One of our tourists is seriously ill. / Some of the tourists don't feel very well.

We should send him to the hospital nearby for medication.

Please call an ambulance immediately.

Is there any doctor or nurse who can speak Chinese?

Step 2 Describing symptoms of the sick tourist to doctor.

What are his symptoms?

What's wrong with her? / What's the problem with her?

He sweats and feels shivery / chilly / dizzy / cold / nauseous / like throwing up.

He got a sharp / splitting pain in his belly.

She has a headache / stomachache / sore throat / cough.

He has a diarrhea / runny nose / chill / high blood pressure / heart attack.

He is running a fever and keeps sneezing.

He felt down and sprained his ankle / broke his leg.

She is having difficulty in breathing.

His itching is unbearable.

He has induced vomiting.

Step 3 Medical treatment.

I'll examine her blood.

They should have some medical tests first.

Let's take his temperature. Tell him to open his mouth.

I want you to have an X-ray taken.

I'll give her a shot / an injection.

He needs to wear a cast.

The patient should be hospitalized and needs to have an operation.

It's not serious. Tell him to take the medicine three times a day, two pills a time and drink plenty of hot water.

Sample Dialogue

(A = Tour Leader; B = John, Local Guide; C = Doctor)

A: John, some of the tourists don't feel very well.

B: What' wrong with them?

A: After dinner, they sweat and feel shivery, and got a sharp pain in their bellies.

B: I'm afraid that they are suffering from food poisoning.

A: I think we should send them to the hospital nearby for medication. Please call an ambulance immediately.

B: All right. I'll do it at once and report it to my company.

...

C: What's the problem with them?

A: Doctor, we are a tour group from China. Some of our guests feel chilly and have got splitting pain in their bellies.

C: Did they vomit?

A: Yes, some of them have induced vomiting. ②

C: What did they have for dinner?

A: They had seafood this evening, like shrimps, crabs, raw lobsters and oysters.

C: They should have some medical tests first.

B: All right. Let's go with them.

...

B: Doctor, here are the test results.

C: Let me see. It's the food poisoning. The seafood they had was not clean.

A: Is it serious?

C: Not very serious. But let me give them injections first. Then I'll write out a prescription for you. Take it to the pharmacy to get the medicine. And tell them to take the medicine three times a day, two pills a time and drink plenty of hot water. After having a rest for two or three days, they will recover soon.

A: Thank you, doctor. Can you make out a diagnosis certificate for the food poisoning for us? With the certificate, we can sue the restaurant and claim damages from the insurance company. [3]

C: Of course, sir.

A and B: Thank you very much.

Ⅲ. Passport Lost

Procedure and Useful Patterns

Step 1 Passport getting lost.

John, Mr. Zhang has got a trouble. He lost his passport.

He is sure his passport was lost. He has checked everywhere but still couldn't find it.

Please check once more. You may have left it somewhere.

Step 2 Claiming for lost passport.

Where can we make a claim for lost passport?

We should go to your travel agency and the police station for certificates for the loss of the passport.

My passport was lost. Could I have it registered?

A lost report, please.

Do you remember when and where you last saw it?

What is the expiration date on your passport?

Step 3 Getting a replacement of passport.

Please go to your embassy or consulate for a replacement and contact the Immigration Bureau for your visa.

Sample Dialogue

(A = Tour Leader; B = John, Local Guide; C = Policeman)

A: John, Mr. Zhang has got a trouble. He lost his passport.

B: I'm sorry to hear that. Are you sure his passport was lost?

A: Yes, he has checked everywhere but still couldn't find it.

B: In this case, we should help him make a claim for lost passport[4].

A: Where can we make a claim for lost passport?

B: Ask Mr. Zhang to go with us to the local police station for certificates for the loss of the passport.

A: OK. Let's go.

...

B: Excuse me, sir.

C: Yes, what can I do for you?

A: Sir, we are a tour group from China. I'm the tour leader. This gentleman is a member of my group. He lost his passport. Could he have it registered?

C: (To Mr. Zhang) Do you remember when and where you last saw it?

A: He said he saw it in his pocket this morning when he was having breakfast in the hotel.

C: (To Mr. Zhang) Could you please tell me your name, passport number and the expiration date on your passport?

A: Oh, sir. I have made photocopies of the passports of the whole group. Let me see. Oh, yes. Here it is.

C: I see. Please fill out this form.

A: All right. (Help Mr. Zhang filling out the form) Here you are.

C: Here's the certificate for the loss of the passport.

A: Thank you, sir.

C: It's my pleasure.

...

A: John, what should we do next?

B: I'll accompany you to your embassy for a replacement and contact the Immigration Bureau for visa.

A: You are most helpful. Thank you so much.

B: Don't mention it. Shall we go now?

Ⅳ. Traffic Accident

Procedure and Useful Patterns

Step 1 Calling the police and asking for help.

Hello. Is that the police station? We are in a traffic accident near the Central Park.

The accident is at the intersection of 50th Avenue and Park Road.

There is an injured person here. Please give him first aid.

I can't move. Please call an ambulance.

She is seriously injured. She broke her arm. Could you take her to the hospital?

Step 2 Report the process of the whole accident.

The car suddenly came at us from the side at the intersection.

We were stopped at a red light. A car hit our bus from behind and drove away.

I was in too much shock. I didn't see the car's plate.

Step 3 Contact the insurance company (contact your embassy or consulate if necessary).

Sample Dialogue

(A = Tour Leader; B = Policeman)

A: Hello. Is that the police station?

B: Yes. What can I do for you?

A: We are in a traffic accident.

B: Where did it happen?

A: It is near the Central Park.

B: Anyone injured?

A: Yes. There is an injured person here. Please call an ambulance.

B: Please remain calm and keep the scene intact. We'll get there in five minutes.

...

B: Get the injured into the ambulance and send him to the hospital. Who called the police just now?

A: It was me.

B: Your driver license, please.

A: Sorry, sir. I'm not the driver. I'm the tour leader of a tour group from China.

B: Where is the driver?

A: He is seriously injured. He broke his leg. He is in the ambulance on the way to the hospital.

B: I see. What happened here? Would you please give us a detailed account of the accident?

A: OK. We were on our way back to the hotel. Our bus was stopped by a red light at the intersection.[⑤] A truck suddenly rushed at us from the side at the intersection and hit the front part of our bus and drove away.

B: Did you see the truck's plate?

A: I'm sorry. I was in too much shock. ⑥

B: Did you see the color or the model?

A: I don't know the model. And the color is white. I'm quite sure.

B: Can you show me your passport?

A: Sure. Here you are.

B: Well, that's all I have to ask you. This is your statement I have taken down. Read it and make a correction if you find anything incorrect.

A: OK. Everything is correct.

B: Please sign it here. Thank you for your cooperation.

Notes

① cell phone 手机

② ... some of them have induced vomiting. ……他们当中有些人已经吐了。

③ With the certificate, we can sue the restaurant and claim damages from the insurance company. 有了那个证明,我们就可以起诉餐馆并向保险公司索赔。

④ make a claim for lost passport 申请护照遗失

⑤ Our bus was stopped by a red light at the intersection. 我们的巴士在十字路口等红灯。

⑥ I was in too much shock. 我刚才被惊呆了。

Words and Expressions

emergency	*n.* 紧急情况;急诊
smoothly	*adv.* 顺利地;平稳地
considerate	*adj.* 体贴的;考虑周详的
ambulance	*n.* 救护车
shivery	*adj.* 发抖的
chilly	*adj.* 发冷的
dizzy	*adj.* 头晕的
nauseous	*adj.* 恶心的
itching	*n.* 痒

unbearable	*adj.* 难以忍受的
injection	*n.* 注射;打针
crab	*n.* 蟹
lobster	*n.* 龙虾
oyster	*n.* 牡蛎,蚝
prescription	*n.* 处方
diagnosis	*n.* 诊断
sue	*v.* 起诉
expiration	*n.* 截止期
replacement	*n.* 更换补发的护照
intersection	*n.* 十字路口
injured	*adj.* 受伤的
plate	*n.* 车牌;牌照

throw up	呕吐
splitting pain	绞痛
have a diarrhea	拉肚子
runny nose	流鼻涕
keep sneezing	一直打喷嚏
sprain one's ankle	扭了脚踝
induce vomiting	催吐
wear a cast	打石膏
Immigration Bureau	移民局
first aid	急救
keep the scene intact	保护现场
driver license	驾驶证

Assignments

Translate the following into English.

(1) 我要你去拍一张 X 光片。

(2) 他昨天晚上又拉肚子又呕吐,现在感觉头晕。

(3) 我的护照可能掉在银行了。

(4) 她的腿断了,动不了,请给她急救。

(5) 我吓呆了,根本没有看清楚那辆车的牌号。

In-class Practice

Role-play

Divide the class into groups to make a conversation according to the situation given below:

One of the tourists in your group is telling you that he feels cold, and has a sore throat, headache, high fever. You accompany him to the hospital.

Broaden Your Mind

Top Tourist Attractions in Australia

Australia is the fifth largest country in the world, and the smallest and driest continent. It is also the lowest stretch of flat land. The largest part of its vast unknown has been tamed, and the deserts do not look so wild anymore. The continent is a beautiful paradise, filled with deserts, tropical forests, mountains, an abundance of plants and unique animals like the Koala bear and the Kangaroo. The main attractions consist of a series of national parks, lush forests, museums and galleries.

National parks are probably the best tourist attractions in Australia. One such park is the Blue Mountain Reserve, which is situated 81 kilometers West of Sydney, in the New South Wales region. Geographically the park is located in an area of high plateaus which are crossed by numerous rivers and valleys. The highest mountain in the area is Mount Werong, which is also an interesting destination for hikers.

If you are looking for natural tourist attractions in Australia, you should definitely visit Fraser Island. It is the biggest sand island in the world, situated on the eastern coast in the state of Queensland. It is also part of the UNESCO Patrimony. The relief of the island has many by sweet water lakes, colored sand stones, a rich tropical forest, rivers and white sandy beaches.

The Sydney Opera House, built near the promontory of Bennelong has become the symbol of the city and one of the most popular attractions in Australia. Every year, the country is visited by art lovers, who come specially to visit this unique monument. The structure was designed by the Danish architect Jorn Utzon, and it is built in a modernist style. It contains six auditoriums which house operas, theaters, and ballet shows. There is also an open air amphitheater for outdoor representations.

The great coral reef is the most famous marine protected area, and it is part of the UNESCO Patrimony. It stretches over 2, 300 kilometers across the north eastern coastline, from Bundanber to Cap York. The Great Coral Reef Barrier is the largest coral reef system in the world, which houses over 400 different types of corals, 1,500 species of fish and 4,000 species of mollusks.

Tasmania is the smallest state of Australia, situated on the island with the same name. It is separated from the mainland by the Bass Strait. It is formed mainly by pristine landscapes, abandoned beaches, mountains and 17 national parks. It is one of the best attractions in Australia for intrepid travelers. If you are the kind of person who likes being in touch in nature you should know that Tasmania is well known for its extremely clean atmosphere. There is something for anyone here. In the regions of the central plateaus there are hundreds of lakes, the forests are home to many species of animals and the forgotten beaches have a mystical feel.

One of the biggest attractions is the feeling of total isolation. In Australia it is very easy to find an abandoned beach or an isolated corner in the woods. Water sports are extremely popular, and for those of you who are in love with nature, Australia is the best choice for your next vacation.

Unit 13　Free-day Activities
自由活动日

【内容导读】

本单元介绍在国外旅游期间，领队如何帮助游客解决在自由活动时间出现的问题，包括在自动取款机取款、超市购物退货等。

【学习目标】

熟练掌握在自动取款机取款、超市购物退货等程序及常用用语与句型。

【学习要点】

购物退货的问题描述及换货与退货要求的英语表述。

Text

During the tour abroad, there will be free-time activities arranged for the tourists. In most cases, the tour leader goes with the tourists to help them with interpretation. As a tour leader, you must be familiar with the country or the city visited by the tour group, including the culture and folk customs, the law, and the local public services, such as transportation, restaurants, banking service, mail service, and even medication. In free-day activities, the tour leader must assure the safety of the tourists. Do not encourage them to participate in dangerous activities.

Oral Skills

Ⅰ. Drawing Money at ATM[1]

Procedure and Useful Patterns

Step 1　Asking for help.

I just want to know if I can draw some money from the ATM by my Union Pay card[2].

I really don't know how to handle it, either.

Would you please show me how to take money from the ATM?

Step 2　Drawing money by instructions on the screen.

It's easy. Do as you are instructed.

When your password is admitted, just push the Withdraw button to withdraw cash.

You are only allowed to take up to 1,000 dollars each time.

Sample Dialogue

(A = Tour Leader; B = Bank Clerk)

A: Excuse me, madam.

B: Yes. What can I do for you?

A: I'm a tour leader. Some members of my tour group want to get some dollars in cash. I just want to know if we can draw some money from the ATM by Union Pay card.

B: Please have a look at the upper part of the ATM. If there is the logo of Union Pay, that means, it is accepted.

A: I see. Oh, yes. There it is. But I really don't know how to handle it. Can you show me how to take money from the ATM?

B: It's easy. Do as you are instructed. ③ First, insert your card into the slot. When the screen shows "enter password", enter your password. Then, when your password is admitted, just push the Withdraw button to withdraw cash. Finally, enter the number of the amount you want to take, your money is drawn.

A: What is the Balance button for?

B: It is for checking the balance in your account. ④

A: How much can I take from it at a time?

B: You are only allowed to take up to 1,000 dollars each time. If you want to take 2,000, for instance, that means you'll have to withdraw twice.

A: All right. I'll remember the instruction. Thank you for your help.

B: You are welcome.

Ⅱ. Refunding Purchase at a Shop

Procedure and Useful Patterns

Step 1　Telling the shop assistant the problem.

This lady bought this camera here yesterday, but it doesn't work.

When pushing this button, nothing happens.

This T-shirt I bought here this morning is small, I can not wear.

Do you have the receipt with you?

Would you please show me the receipt?

Step 2 Asking for changing or refunding purchase.

Can I change it for a bigger one?

I just want to get my money back.

I just want another camera like the one I bought.

You can just pay the difference.

Sample Dialogue

(A = Tour Leader; B = Shop Assistant)

A: Excuse me, miss.

B: Yes. May I help you?

A: This lady bought this camera here yesterday, but it doesn't work.

B: I'm sorry to hear that. What's the problem?

A: Something might be wrong with this button. When pushing it, nothing happens.

B: Let me see. Yes, you are right. Can you show me the receipt?

A: Yes. Here it is.

B: All right. Do you want to change for another one or... ?

A: She just want another camera like the one she bought. Can you find her another one?

B: Let me see if I can find another one. Oh, here's one. It's almost the same but the price is a little bit higher.

A: How much is this one?

B: It's 186 dollars. You can just pay the difference.

A: (Turn to the tourist and ask for her idea) It's 24 dollars more than she had paid. And she doesn't like the black color. She likes a purple one.

B: OK. I'll try to find a purple one. I'm sorry. We don't have a purple one and we don't have another camera like that.

A: All right. Then she just wants to get her money back.

B: OK. Sorry we can't give you the right one. Would you please sign here? Thanks. Here is your money.

A: Thank you.

Notes

① ATM（Automatic Teller Machine）自动取款机
② Union Pay card（中国）银联卡
③ Do as you are instructed. 按指令操作。
④ It is for checking the balance in your account. 它是用来核查账户余额的。

Words and Expressions

interpretation	*n.* 口译
withdraw	*v.*（从银行）取（钱）
password	*n.* 密码；口令
logo	*n.* 标识；标志
balance	*n.* 余额
instruction	*n.* 指南
refund	*v.* 退款；退货
difference	*n.* 差价；差额
draw money	取钱；提款
participate in	参加
up to	多达；不多于；一直到

Assignments

Translate the following into English.
（1）请问我能用中国银联卡从自动取款机取现金吗？
（2）你一次最多可以取 1000 欧元。
（3）这件衣服紧了一点，我能换一件大点的吗？
（4）请问，你们有便宜一些的吗？
（5）如果你们不能找到跟我买的一样的手表，我要求退货。

In-class Practice

Role-play

Divide the class into groups to make a conversation according to the situation given below:

You found that the handbag you bought in the shop is of poor quality. You want to get your money back.

Broaden Your Mind

Getting Around in London

When you first arrive in London, pick up a free tourist map at any transport ticket offices, tourist/information centers and hotels. If you would like to have a comprehensive map showing all streets of the London area, buy an A-Z London Street Atlas, available from most news agents and bookshops.

Check out our airport transfer guide for transport from airports to central London. Many hotels have shuttles that take you to their hotels in central London. There are also bus services to major hotels and drop-off locations.

The quickest way of getting around in London is by London Underground (i. e., subway, also called the "Tube" in the U. K.). London has one of the most comprehensive underground systems in the world (and also the oldest in the world, built 120 years ago). The tube runs from 5:30 a. m. to midnight Mon-Sat, and from 7:00 a. m. to 11:30 p. m. Sun. During the rush hours (8-9:30 a. m., 5-6:30 p. m., Mon-Sat), the tube can be very crowded.

There are 11 tube lines, each has its own name and color on the tube map. On most platforms, there are information displays showing the destination and due time of the next train. Some of the tube line (e. g., northern line) has two branches, and the displays also show which branch the train is going to (e. g., Morden Via Bank means the train goes to Morden via the Bank station).

London also has an extensive bus network (over 17,000 bus stops all over London). However, it is often difficult to know when you should get off if you do not know the area well. After midnight, night buses are the only public transport in London. All night buses have the prefix N and most of them start from Trafalgar Square.

Discover Amsterdam

What makes Amsterdam so attractive is the 17th century historical atmosphere combined with the mentality of a modern metropolis creating a friendly and relaxed environment. The small scale of the buildings and the intimacy of the streets, canals and squares create an atmosphere that visitors find unique.

The city has the highest museum density in the world and is home to cultural highlights, such as the Van Gogh Museum, Anne Frank House, Hermitage Amsterdam and the Rijksmuseum with Rembrandt's world-famous nightwatch. Other well known places of interest in Amsterdam are the Palace on the Dam, the Artis Zoo, Jewish Historical Museum and the Rembrandt House.

When in Paris, visit the Eiffel Tower. When in Barcelona, visit the Sagrada Familia. And when you are in Amsterdam, you should definitely experience a tour of the city's famous canals. Take a canal tour of Amsterdam and discover the historical canal district which was added to the UNESCO World Heritage List in 2011. You will see the most beautiful canal houses with staircases, where the number of steps demonstrates the resident's status. In other words, a beautiful tour filled with interesting facts about Amsterdam. While it may seem like a tourist attraction, it is a wonderful experience that will teach you a lot about the history of Amsterdam.

The best way to get around Amsterdam is on a bike. You won't become any more local than by cycling around Amsterdam. However, you can also book a package. There are night tours by candle light. You can hire an entire boat, and so on. Whatever you decide, make sure you include a canal tour in your Amsterdam trip because Amsterdam is at its most beautiful seen from the water.

Part Ⅲ

Practical English Writing for Travel

实用旅游英文写作

Unit 14 Travel Information
旅游咨询

【内容导读】

本单元首先从英文商务信函写作格式与排列方法开始，通过实例介绍各类旅游信息咨询信函及回复信函的写作格式和内容，以及英文表达方式和常用句型。

【学习目标】

通过本单元学习，熟练掌握英语旅游咨询及其回复信件的写作格式、内容、写作要点及常用句型，并能熟练拟写咨询及回复信件。熟练掌握游客及电话咨询口语技能。

【学习要点】

(1)咨询及回复信件常用句型：

Could you please send me all available information about...?

We would be appreciating/grateful/happy if you could send me....

Please send me information on....

We here enclose a copy of....

(2)咨询口语技能。

Text

In order to find happy feeling of spiritual and ease the pressure from life and work, people always like to travel in their spare time. ① However, things always do not happen as people's wishes, not all travelers can feel the pleasure from the travel because they don't clearly understand travel-related information, resulting in a blind travel. But such situations can be avoided if you prefer to ask the travel agency for information about travel.

Travel service, like other enterprises of tourism industry; usually receive letters or phone calls from tourists for travel information, like the touring routes, prices, flights, accommodations, and even shopping, recreation and business facilities. As a working staff, you need to learn to read these letters and write replies as requested.

Ⅰ. Business Letters

Format and Contents

① The heading.

② The inside address.

Receiver's address, below the date line.

③ The salutation.

Dear Sir or Madam, / Dear Sirs, / Dear Gentlemen, / To Whom It May Concern,

④ The body of the letter.

⑤ The complimentary close.

Yours faithfully, / Yours truly, / Yours respectfully,

⑥ The signature.

The signature's position or title could be marked below.

⑦ The reference line.

⑧ Initials.

⑨ Enclosure.

Encl. / Enc. If the enclosures are posted separately, it should be....

Encl. Under separate cover

Sample

Editorial Department of China Scenic Spots and Historical Sites Vision
149 Ruishan Road Hechuan Chongqing 401520
Tel: 023-42823529 Fax: 023-42823532

Date
Ref.
Inside Address
Dear Sirs,

____
______________ body ______________
____
____

Yours faithfully,

Encl.

Ⅱ. Letters for Information

1. Requirements.

(1) Open and direct;

(2) Simple and brief.

2. Format and contents.

(1) Salutation;

(2) State your purpose.

The purpose for such a letter is to ask for travel information. In the letter you just directly ask the receiver to provide you what you need and want. You may use the following patterns to express your purpose:

We should be most grateful if you would send me....

We would be appreciating if you send us... as early as possible.

I'll be very glad if you send me....

I would be happy to get any available information about....

Could you please send me all available information on...?

Could you let me know...?

Please send me information on....

3. Express thanks.

To express your thanks, you may use:

Thank you for your early reply.

We are looking forward to your early reply.

Thank you in advance.

Best wishes.

Sample 1

Feb. 15, 2003
China International Travel Service
Chongqing Branch Chongqing 400013
P. R. China
Dear Sirs,
I've learnt that Chongqing is a well-known tourist destination in China. My family and I intend to come to Chongqing for a holiday in spring. We are especially interested in the Yangtze River Gorges. ② We would be most grateful if you could send me brochures of the Three Gorges as well as lists of recommended hotels. Could you also let me know what fares are by air or by train, if we'd like to go to Chongqing from Beijing?
Thank you for your early reply.
Yours faithfully,
×××

Sample 2

> Dear Gentlemen,
>
> Will you please send me all available information on your organized tours[③] of Singapore, Malaysia and Thailand, including the fares, itinerary, transportation, meals, accommodation, etc.?
>
> This will help me much in deciding where to spend my two-week holiday.
>
> Best wishes.
>
> Yours truly,
>
> ×××

Sample 3

> Dear Sir or Madam,
>
> I'm a Canadian tourist. I'd like to tour the Three Gorges.
>
> I'll be very glad if you send me details of your sailing from Chongqing to Yichang at the end of July, and of fares payable for first-class cabin. I would also be happy to get any available information about the ships scheduled to sail for Yichang during this period.
>
> Thank you very much for your early reply.
>
> Yours sincerely,
>
> *Brad Laycer*

Ⅲ. A Reply Letter

If you receive a letter for information, you need to write back in time, telling the guest if you can provide the service he or she asked.

Format and Contents

1. Express thanks.

Thank you for your letter of / dated Feb. 20.

Thank you for your letter of... / asking for information about / on....

In reply to your letter of..., we enclose a copy of....

Your letter dated... has been received. We are very glad to know that you want to / we feel honored that you want to....

2. Reply.

(1) Repeat the guest's requirements and tell them if you can provide the service.

(2) Enclosure.

(3) Wishes.

We here enclose a copy of. . . .

We enclose with this letter a. . . .

For your reference we enclose a. . . .

We are now making the following offers.

We can offer you the following. . . .

If you need further help, please contact me/do contact us.

For any additional information, please contact us.

We'll be glad to offer other information on further request.

We look forward to your booking.

We are looking forward to seeing you at. . . .

Sample 1

> Dear Mr. Mike,
>
> Your letter dated 18th Jan. has been received. We are very glad to know that you want to tour Chongqing. We here enclose a brochure of the Three Gorges and a list of recommended hotels for your reference. If you come to Chongqing from Beijing by air, it will cost you about \$ 150. If you travel by train, the cost will be about \$ 60 for a first class seat.
>
> If you need further help, please contact me.
>
> Yours truly,
>
> ×××

Sample 2

Dear Miss Linda,

In reply to your letter of October 10, we enclose a copy of itinerary of Hong Kong, Macao and Thailand. As the ten-day tour of Hong Kong, Macao and Thailand is a hot route especially during the traditional Chinese Spring Festival holidays, we strongly suggest that you make a reservation with us 15 days in advance. ④

For any additional information, please contact us.

We look forward to your booking.

Yours truly,

×××

Sample 3

Dear Brad Laycer,

Thank you for your letter of July 1 asking for information about sailing from Chongqing to Yichang.

We here enclose a copy of our S. S. Marcopolo⑤ sailing list in which you will find details of sailing and fares of different classes, including excursion fares. As our responsibility for baggage is limited under the term of the passenger ticket, we strongly urge passengers to insure against all risks for full period of their journey. In addition, all foreign passengers are required to carry a valid passport issued by their own countries.

We'll be glad to offer other information on further request.

Yours truly,

×××

Oral Skills

Asking for Information—At a Travel Agent's

Procedure and Useful Patterns

Step 1 Saying hello and offering help.

Good morning. Can I help you?

What can I do for you?

Step 2 Guest's requests for information.

I want to go to ... for a holiday.

We plan to tour ....

I'd like to get from you the ....

Do you have any tour including ...?

Can you arrange a trip for us?

Step 3 Asking the guest for details.

(1) For destination/tour route.

What places do you prefer to go?

Do you have any idea of what places to go?

What are you interested in?

We particularly want to visit ....

We want to see the places of interest in ....

Can you arrange such a tour for us?

(2) For tour period.

How long would you like to stay in ...?

How long will the tour be?

How long is your holiday?

How long would you like your trip?

Well, three days.

I can only be away for a week for a trip.

(3) For tour fares.

How much is the tour? And what does it include?

How much do you usually charge for a tour of ...?

What is the fee of guide per day?

What is the price of the tour?

2,000 *for each person, including ....*

That depends. It's usually around 2,000 *dollars, including....*

Step 4 Making introduction and suggestion.

Here are the brochures that describing various tour routes in .... You can choose anyone you like.

We have (there is) a three-day package tour. You will have 3 *full days in.... It is a general tour of .... The itinerary includes the places of interest such as....*

The tour includes....

Can I recommend the ... tour to you? These places are worth seeing.

Would you like to take a package tour or travel alone?

We suggest you join the group. That would be fun to share the sights with others.

Step 5 Expressing thanks.

Well, the information is very helpful. Thank you very much.

Thank you for your information. Goodbye.

You are welcome. Goodbye.

Sample Dialogue 1

Clerk: Good morning. Can I help you?

Guest: Good morning. My wife and I, together with our two sons want to go to China for a two-week holiday. Can you arrange a trip for us?

Clerk: Sure. What places do you prefer to go?

Guest: We especially want to visit Beijing, Xi'an, the Yangtze River Gorges and Shanghai. Do you have any tour including all these places?

Clerk: Yes, we have. Here are the brochures that describe various tour routes in China. You can choose anyone you like.

Guest: How much do you usually charge for a tour of China?

Clerk: That depends. ⑥ It's usually around 2,000 dollars, including fees for transportation, accommodation and admission for places of interest. The brochures will give you details.

Guest: Oh, good. The information is very useful. Thanks a lot. Goodbye.

Clerk: You're welcome. Goodbye.

Sample Dialogue 2

Clerk: Hello, China Travel Service Hong Kong. Can I help you?

Guest: Yes, I'd like to get from you some information about your tour to Shenzhen, Guangzhou and Zhuhai. Can you arrange such a tour for us?

Clerk: Sure. But how long would you like to stay in these cities?

Guest: Well, three days.

Clerk: OK, we have a 3-day package tour. You will have 3 full days in the cities. It's a general tour of the cities. The itinerary includes the places of interest like Window of the World, China Folk Culture Village, and Gongbei Market⑦.

Guest: That sounds good. How much is the tour?

Clerk: 2,000RMB for each person.

Guest: And what does it include?

Clerk: Well, it's a package tour, so everything is included, like the transportation fares, hotel accommodation, meals and sightseeing.

Guest: Great! Thank you for the information. Goodbye.

Clerk: Welcome. Goodbye

Notes

① In order to find happy feeling of spiritual and ease the pressure from life and work, people always like to travel in their spare time. 为了寻求幸福,缓解生活和工作的压力,人们总是喜欢在空闲时间旅行。

② We are especially interested in the Yangtze River Gorges. 我们尤其对长江三峡感兴趣。

③ organized tours 组团游

④ ... we strongly suggest that you make a reservation with us 15 days in advance. ……我们强烈建议你提前 15 天向我方预订。

⑤ S. S. Marcopolo 马可波罗号游轮

⑥ That depends. 看情况而定。

⑦ Window of the World, China Folk Culture Village, and Gongbei Market 世界之窗、中国民族文化村和拱北市场

Words and Expressions

information	*n.* 信息,咨询
format	*n.* 格式
appreciating	*adj.* 感激的,感谢的
grateful	*adj.* 感激的,感谢的
available	*adj.* 可得到的,可买到的,可能的
destination	*n.* 目的地
brochure	*n.* (宣传用)画册,手册
recommended	*adj.* 推荐的
itinerary	*n.* 游程,游览安排
fare	*n.* 费用
accommodation	*n.* 住宿
schedule	*n.* 时刻表,日期表
enclose	*vt.* 附
additional	*adj.* 另外的,额外的
urge	*vt.* 奉劝,劝告,建议
valid	*adj.* 有效的
look forward to	期待,期盼
in advance	提前,预先
for your reference	供参考
hot route	热点线路,热线
make a reservation with	向…预订

Assignments

1. Write a letter according to the following conditions.

某公司决定在你方5星级游船上举行董事会议(boarding conference)。发来传真询问能否提供并安排:

(1) 6间标准舱、1间套房;

(2) 会议室一间(人数:13人)。

时间:9月3—6日。

请及时回复并提供报价。

2. Translate the following into English.

(1) 如蒙寄送有关长江三峡介绍画册,将不胜感激。

(2) 请提供有关新(加坡)马(来西亚)泰(国)10 日游的信息,谢谢。

(3) 你们提供的信息将有助于我们作出到哪里去度假的决策。

(4) 我们建议你提前 10 天向我方预订。

(5) 随信附上行程单一份,供你方参考。

In-class Practice

Role-play

This is Tom's first visit to Chongqing. Tomorrow he'll be off. He wants to go sightseeing around the city. But he doesn't know where to go, what to see, and how to get there. Work in pairs. Ask and give your partner information. Try to use the following expressions:

I'd like the city tour, but I really don't know...?

Are there any places of interest in...?

What are you interested in?

Is there anything special?

Can you arrange such a tour for me?

Can I recommend the ... tour to you?

How much is the tour?

And what does it include?

Broaden Your Mind

Travel Tips

Travel is a happy thing in our life, but during the trip, we will inevitably encounter many difficulties and problems, making the journey no longer easy. So, if you want to get more satisfactory travel, you should choose a suitable way to travel and tourist destination, know and master the relevant travel tips. Arranging travel schedule are the most important steps before traveling.

1. Choose tourism way

Tourism ways is divided into three parts: travel with tour groups, travel with family and friends, personal self-tourism. Choosing what kind of way is mainly based on your own need, but it should fully take into account personal interests, hobbies, economic, time and other aspects of actual situation. Different tourism, different travel content will bring you substantial experience and a great temptation.

2. Preparation before travel

Before travel, you should seriously consider the travel partners, destinations, economic costs, the physical condition of individuals and others, and then refer to the travel destination's transportation, accommodation, climate and other conditions. To make a practical plan, meanwhile, the budget is also necessary, such as lodging, food fees and lastly to make a luggage table, including personal documents, medicines.

3. Apply for travel documents

When traveling internationally, it is imperative that you research the passport and visa requirements of your destination countries prior to departure. Depending on your country of origin and arrival, a passport and visa may be required to enter the country, and understanding the difference between and purpose of each will make the amount of time spent in the customs line as minimal as possible.

A passport is a universally accepted international document that is sufficient for crossing the border and provides a person's identity and nationality. It is issued by the traveler's country of origin and provides proof of citizenship.

A visa is a document granting permission for entry into a country to fulfill a specific purpose. A visa is granted by the country the traveler is visiting and is typically stamped into the traveler's passport.

Unit 15 Reservation and Confirmation
预订与确认

【内容导读】

本单元介绍旅游预订信件与预订确认信件，包括旅游线路预订、旅游酒店预订、旅游机票预订等内容。

【学习目标】

掌握各种旅游预订及确认信件的英文写作格式、写作要点及常用句型，并能熟练拟写英文旅游预订及确认信件，熟练掌握预订口语技能。

【学习要点】

预订及确认信件常用句型：

I' d like to book a . . . .

I wish to reserve a . . . .

Would you please arrange the ten-day tour to. . . for us?

Please confirm the booking as soon as payment is made by checks.

Could you please confirm this booking with a return letter?

In reply to your letter of / dated on. . . , we confirm that. . . .

We regret to inform you that . . . is fully booked.

Text

Making reservation, you must indicate the name of the tour route or destination, date, and your requirements for hotels, rooms, meals and transportation, or some other special needs for your trip. If it is a booking for hotel room, you need to indicate the room type, room rate, number of rooms, and date. If it is for air ticket or train ticket, the date, destination, flight number or train number, number of persons, and class should be clearly indicated in your letter.

Ⅰ. A Letter for Reservation

Format and Main Contents

1. Salutation.

2. Your purposes or your requirements.

For reservation, you just tell the travel agency what you want and need. You may use the following useful patterns:

I' d like to make a trip to... from... to.... Would you please arrange the ten-day tour for us?

I' d like to make a reservation for the 3-day package tour to... from... to... for my wife and me.

I wish to reserve one soft berth on the 9:30 train from... to... on Sept. 4.

I' d like to book a seat on Flight... from... to... at 10:30 on... Economy class.

I would like to book a... room with a bath/shower from... to....

3. Asking for confirmation.

Ask the travel agency to write back to confirm your booking. You may use the following useful patterns:

Could you please confirm this booking with a return letter?

We look forward to receiving your confirmation at your earliest convenience.

Please confirm the booking as soon as payment is made by check.

I enclose 50 dollars for reservation fee, and a registered and stamped envelope with return address.

Sample 1

Dear Sirs,

My wife and I would like to make a trip to Chongqing and the Three Gorges in China from May 1 to May 10. Would you please arrange the ten-day tour for us according to the itinerary enclosed and the following items?

(1) Room required: 1 double room with a bath.

(2) Hotels: 3-star hotel.

(3) Steamer: standard cabin on deluxe cruiser for traveling on the Yangtze River.

(4) Meals: American breakfast daily, Chinese food for lunch and supper.

Enclosed with a check of $ 1500 for the reservation fee.

We look forward to receiving your confirmation at your earliest convenience.

Yours faithfully,

Smith

Sample 2

> Dear Sirs,
> I would like to book a single room with a bath from Sept. 21 to Oct. 2, inclusive. It's for Mr. Andrews, our sales director. We would like you to provide a room with a telephone extension and overlooking the park, if possible. ①
> Mr. Andrews will arrive at your hotel on the morning of Sept. 21, and leave in the afternoon on Oct. 2. Could you please confirm this booking with a return letter?
> We look forward to hearing from you.
> Yours faithfully,
> ×××

Sample 3

> Dear Gentleman,
> I would like to book a seat on Flight CA 986 departing from Beijing at 19:00 on Friday October 2 and arriving at San Francisco Airport, economy class. The passenger is Yoder J. Bruce, passport number.... Please confirm this booking as soon as payment is made by check.
> Yours faithfully,
> ×××

Ⅱ. A Letter for Confirmation

Format and Main Contents

1. Salutation.

2. Confirmation.

Repeat the guest's requests and assure the guest that you can offer the services needed by the guest. If you can't offer the service the guest asked, you have to reply promptly, and explain the reason why not. It is better to make your suggestion.

You may use the following useful patterns:

Thank you for your letter of..., we are now confirming your booking for....

We are now confirming your ten-day China tour arrangement.

In reply to your letter of..., we confirm that....

We regret (are sorry) to inform you that ... is fully booked, and there is no cancellation at present. We suggest that....

3. Thanks and wishes.

Wish you a wonderful tour in....

Hope you a pleasant journey.

We hope you will enjoy your stay with us.

Sample 1

Dear Mr. Smith,

Thank you for booking with us. We are now confirming your ten-day China tour arrangement. All your tour arrangements with our travel service are now in order. Enclosed are your itinerary and necessary coupons.

Your journey starts at 9:00 a.m. on May 1, from Chongqing Hotel. We'll meet you and your wife at the lobby of the hotel at 8:50 a.m.

Wish you a wonderful tour in China.

Yours sincerely,

×××

(manager of sales department)

Sample 2

Dear Mr. Andrews,

In reply to your letter of Sept. 5, we confirm that we have reserved for you for the period from Sept. 21 to Oct. 2. One single room with a bath and a telephone extension, over the park, at the rate of $ 60 per day, service, tax and all charges included. The room will be ready by 10 o'clock on Sept. 21.

We hope you will enjoy your stay with us and we are looking forward to welcoming you.

Yours sincerely,

×××

Dear Mr. Andrews,
Thank you for booking with us. We are sorry to inform you that we cannot provide you a single room with a bath. Because we are fully booked for the period from Sept. 21 to Oct. 2, and there is no cancellation at present. ②
If you would like to (we suggest that you) change your date a few days later, say Sept. 25, we then have rooms available for you. ③ Otherwise, we suggest that you book with Hilton Hotel which is not far from our hotel, there may be rooms available.
Yours faithfully,
×××

Sample 3

Dear ×××,
We are now confirming your booking for a seat for Mr. Yoder J. Bruce on Flight CA 986 from Beijing to San Francisco at 19:00 on Friday, October 2, economy class.
Thank you for booking with us. Hope Mr. Yoder a pleasant journey.
Yours faithfully,
×××

Oral Skills

Booking Hotel Rooms

Procedure and Useful Patterns

Step 1 Say hello and offer help.

Good morning, Hilton Hotel. Can I help you?

Step 2 Ask for information from guests.

(For asking for information, you must ask politely, using "could", "would".)

(1) Ask for number of the guest.

For how many? / How many are you? / How many are there in your party?

(2) Ask for date and duration.

OK, but for when, sir? / but for which date, sir? / when do you require the room?

How long do you plan to stay? / How long will you be staying? / For how many nights?

(3) Ask for room type.

What kind of room would you like?

We have double room, connecting room and suite. Which one do you prefer?

Sometimes you need to describe the rooms and tell the guests the room rate. You may use the following expressions:

A ... room is slightly more expensive / cheaper / larger.

All our rooms have got air-conditioning.

Deluxe rooms have a view of the sea / river / mountain.

We have a very nice suite with two bedrooms and a living room. It's very quiet at night and it has a view of the bay.

It's on the 10th floor, overlooking the park / harbor / pool.

We can provide you a double room. It faces the Yangtze River. You can enjoy the magnificent view of the Yangtze.

May I suggest that you try one of our ... rooms? It has a king-size bed and a mini-bar, and it has a beautiful view of the harbor.

The rate for a double room is $60 a night / per night.

The daily rate for this one is $80, and the weekly rate is $500.

It's $ 140 per night including 10% service charge.

Another kind is $50 a night. Which one do you prefer?

(4) Ask for name, passport number and phone number .

Your name and passport number, please.

Could you please tell me your name and passport number?

May I have your name and your passport number?

And your phone number please.

(5) Ask for arriving time and date.

What time do you expect to arrive, sir?

Step 3　Confirmation.

OK, I'd like to confirm your reservation / that's settled. A double room for ... for 5 nights from ... to .... Is that right?

Thank you. We'll mail / E-mail you a reservation card confirming your booking as soon as possible. We are looking forward to seeing you.

Sample Dialogue

Clerk: Good morning. This is room reservation. May I help you?

Guest: Yes, I'd like to book a room, please.

Clerk: OK, but for when, sir?

Guest: For November 11.

Clerk: How long will you stay?

Guest: About a week.

Clerk: What kind of room would you like, sir?

Guest: I'd like a double room for my wife and me. By the way, what's the rate for a double room?

Clerk: It's $ 80 a night, another kind is $ 60 per night. Which one do you like?

Guest: $ 60 a night is OK.

Clerk: Could you please give me your name and your passport number?

Guest: Yes. It's John Hopkins and the number is 012161.

Clerk: How do you spell your name, please?

Guest: J-O-H-N, John and H-O-P-K-I-N-S, Hopkins.

Clerk: Thank you. Your phone number, please?

Guest: 0032-28283456.

Clerk: What time do you expect to arrive, sir?

Guest: Let me see, at about 9 a.m.

Clerk: OK. That's settled. A double room for Mr. and Mrs. John Hopkins for one week from November 11. Is that right?

Guest: Right.

Clerk: Thank you. We look forward to seeing you and your wife.

Notes

① We would like you to provide a room with a telephone extension and overlooking the park, if possible. 如有可能,我们希望你方提供一间带电话分机并能俯瞰花园的房间。

② ... and there is no cancellation at present. ……目前没有人取消预订。

③ If you would like to (we suggest that you) change your date a few days later, say Sept. 25, we then have rooms available for you. 如果你愿意把日期往后推迟几天,比如9月25号,我们就有房间提供给你。

Words and Expressions

reserve	*v.* 预订
reservation	*n.* 预订
confirm	*v.* 确认
confirmation	*n.* 确认
economy	*n.* 经济
itinerary	*n.* 行程,旅行日程
coupon	*n.* 票券;文件
overlook	*v.* 俯视,俯瞰
available	*adj.* 可用的;可获得的;可购得的
cancellation	*n.* 取消
make a reservation	预订
book with...	向…预订
in reply to	作为回复,作为答复;兹复
telephone extension	电话分机
fully booked	订满;预订一空

Assignments

1. Write a letter according to the following conditions.

Lily 小姐来信要求预订 CA986 航班机票一张,但该航班已客满。请回信告知,并建议她乘坐泛美航空公司(Pan American Airways)16:15 的航班(航班号 Flight PA763)。

2. Translate the following into English.

(1) 我想预订 10 月 1 日至 8 日澳大利亚—新西兰 8 日游,2 人。请为我们安排。

(2) 我要预订大床房 1 间,时间:5 月 3—5 日。

(3) 很遗憾,由于春节期间是旅游旺季,我们酒店已经预订满了。

(4) 建议你向芬兰航空公司(Fin Air)预订,该公司可能还有航班飞往伦敦。

(5) 请提前15天向中国国际旅行社预订。

In-class Practice

Role-play

Divide the class into groups to make a conversation according to the following situations:

Situation 1

A tour guide is making a phone call to reserve hotel rooms for the tour group for one night. There are 19 members (17 adults including 5 single males, 2 single females, and 5 couples with 2 babies) in this group.

Situation 2

A tour guide wants to arrange a group dinner for local food for his group at 6:00 p.m. in Paris. But the restaurant is fully booked for the period from 6:00 p.m. to 7:00 p.m.

Broaden Your Mind

Dazu Rock Carvings

The Dazu Rock Carvings are a series of Chinese religious cliff stone in the Dazu area near Chongqing. The steep hillsides contain an exceptional series of five clusters of rock carvings dating from the 9th to 13th centuries (they are the Beishan, Baodingshan, Nanshan, Shimenshan and Shizhuanshan Rock Carvings).

There are more than 70 spots of Cliffside carvings composed of more than 50,000 statues and over 100,000 Chinese characters of inscriptions and epigraphs. They display Chinese famous ancient stone carving art and were listed as a World Heritage Site in 1999.

The earliest rock carvings in Dazu County date back to AD 650, in the early years of the Tang Dynasty, but the main period began in the late 9th century. In 892 Wei Junjing, Prefect of Changzhou, pioneered the carvings at Beishan, and his example was followed after the collapse of the Tang Dynasty. Between 1174 and 1252 the monk Zhao

Zhifeng promoted Tantric Buddhism at Baodingshan and created the only large stone ritual site for this belief, attracting master craftsmen from all over the country.

The carvings are known for their grand scale, aesthetic quality and rich diversity of subject matter as well as for being well preserved. Standing as an example of the highest level of Chinese cave temple art dating from the 9th to 13th centuries, the Dazu Rock Carvings not only underline the harmonious coexistence in China of three different religions, namely Buddhism, Taoism and Confucianism, but also provide material proof that cave temple art has increasingly shed light on everyday life. Large numbers of carvings and written historical materials within the heritage site show the great changes in and development of cave temple art and religious beliefs in China during that period.

The Beishan and the Baodingshan rock carvings are the most famous ones among Dazu Rock Carvings. They are mainly depicting Buddhist statuary, and also display Confucian and Taoist statuary. Baodingshan is a very impressive site 15 km north-east of Longgang Town, on the sides of a U-shaped gorge over 500m above sea level. There are two groups of carvings. The first and smaller group, known as Xiaofowan, is on top of the mountain and closely linked with the Holy Longevity Monastery, built at the same time but later destroyed by fire and rebuilt during the Ming and Qing Dynasties. The second (Dafowan), lies to the west of the monastery. With the integration of the basic doctrines of Buddhism, the ethics of Confucianism, the tenets of rationalism, and Taoism, in many ways the Baodingshan carvings may be considered to represent the acme of Chinese rock sculpture.

Dazu Rock carvings are the model of the art of late grottoes statues in China. They have a grand scale, and show the exquisite art and rich contents. They enjoy equal popularity of Dunhuang Mogao Grottoes, Yungang Grottoes and Longmen Grottoes.

Unit 16 Travel Notice
旅行通知

【内容导读】

本单元主要介绍旅行通知,包括出行通知、催款通知和旅行警示等内容。

【学习目标】

掌握旅行通知信件的写作格式、写作要点及常用句型,并能熟练拟写。

【学习要点】

旅行通知信件常用句型:

All your tour arrangements with our travel service are now in order.

You are required to make your payment immediately.

Text

Travel notice is a written formal information, or notification, or warning about a fact, required to be made by law or imparted by an operation of law. Usually, the travel agency sends in advance a letter of travel notice to tourists in order to give them information about the trip they booked or ask them to do something before the start of a tour. The following is an example of travel notice.

Notice of Travel to Tibet for Foreign Tourists

Foreigners need to get the following ready before you start your trip to Tibet.

Applying for the Travel Permission

A foreigner needs to submit his/her travel period, route (s) to Tibet, travel purpose, name, passport number, occupation, work place, address and contact information to the Tibet Autonomous Regional Tourist Reception Agency via a local travel agency. He/she will go through the confirmation procedures in a short period. Usually, the confirmation letter will be delivered by express to a domestic location in seven days.

Certificates: Passport and Visa

A foreign tourist or mountaineer should bear a native passport and a visa issued by the Chinese Embassy stationed in his/her country, except that tourists from the countries that have signed visa-free agreements with China. ①

Confirmation Letter

Organized oversea travel groups should apply for the letter through the Tibet Autonomous Regional Tourist Reception Agency. Tourists can consult the tour offices of the Tibet Autonomous Regional Tourism Bureau in the places such as Beijing, Chengdu, Xi'an, Shanghai, Xining, Hong Kong SAR, and oversea offices in the countries like Nepal, the U. S. and Japan.

Ⅰ. A Letter Telling Tourists That All Is Ready

Format and Main Contents

1. Inform the guest that everything is ready.

You may use:

All your tour arrangements with our travel service are now in order.

2. Enclosure (itinerary & coupons).

3. Tour start.

You may use:

Your tour starts at... from.... We'll meet you there.

4. Wishes.

You may use:

Wish you a pleasant tour.

Sample

Dear Mr. & Mrs. Fred,

Welcome to China.

Thank you for allowing us, your agent's representatives, to serve you.

All your tour arrangements with our travel service are now in order. Enclosed are your itinerary (2 copies) and necessary coupons.

Your first sightseeing tour starts at 8: 30 a. m. on April 20, from the Holiday Inn Yangtze. We shall meet you at the lobby of the hotel at 8: 00 a. m.

For any additional arrangements or information, please contact me. Enclosed please find my calling card.

Wish you a wonderful tour of China.

Yours truly,

× × ×

Ⅱ. A Letter for Payment

Format and Main Contents

1. Tell the guest that we haven't received the payment.

You may use:

So far we don't appear to have received your payment for.... Up today we still haven't received your payment for....

We invite/draw your attention to the fact that your payment for... has not reached us in spite of our repeated requests.

May we remind you that your payment for... has not reached us yet?

2. Urging payment.

You may use:

You are required to make your payment immediately; otherwise, we'll have to cancel your reservation in order to avoid more unnecessary cost.

If your payment fails to reach us by..., we may regretfully think that you have given up your tour plan/ we may be forced to cancel the arrangement for your reservation.

Your tour fares must be paid by..., if you can not do so, then we must regretfully cancel your tour arrangement.

Sample

Dear Mr. Smith,

So far we still haven't received your payment for your ten-day tour of China. If your payment fails to reach us by April 18, we may regretfully think that you have given up your tour plan, and in order to avoid more unnecessary cost, we may be forced to cancel the tour arrangement for your reservation.

In accordance with the relative agreement, your deposit will not be returned to you.

Yours faithfully,

×××

Ⅲ. Travel Warning

Ebola Virus Disease Outbreak

The Department of Health advises travelers to avoid unnecessary travel to Equator province② of the Democratic Republic of Congo, Guinea, Liberia, Nigeria and Sierra Leone.

For further details, please see

Ebola Virus Disease related information (Updated: 19/9/2014) NEW

If you are traveling to West Africa, please make sure to do the following:

- Practice careful hygiene. Avoid contact with blood and body fluids of people who are sick with Ebola.
- Do not handle items that may have come in contact with an infected person's blood or body fluids.
- Avoid funeral or burial rituals that require handling the body of someone who has died from Ebola.
- Avoid contact with wild animals and with raw or undercooked meat (bushmeat).
- Avoid hospitals where Ebola patients are being treated.
- Seek medical care immediately if you develop fever (greater than 101.5℉ or 38.6℃) and additional symptoms such as severe headache, muscle pain, vomiting, diarrhea, stomach pain, or unexplained bleeding or bruising.③

Oral Skills

Change of Schedule

Procedure and Useful Patterns

Step 1 Draw the guests' attention.

Ladies and gentlemen, your attention please. I'm talking about the schedule for today.

I hope you can spare me some time to talk about the itinerary for today.

Step 2 Inform the guests of schedule changed.

There is a little change for today's schedule.

I'm sorry. We have to change our schedule for today because of the bad weather.

As you can see, it is raining heavily. We have to change into an indoor activity today.

Sample Dialogue

(G = Guide; T = Tourist)

G: Ladies and gentlemen, your attention please. I'm talking about the schedule for today.

T: Is there any change?

G: Yes, there is a little change for today's schedule. According to the itinerary, we are going to the zoo to see the panda bears. But I'm sorry. As you can see, it is raining heavily outside. And the weather forecast says it will not stop until this evening. So we have to change into an indoor activity.

T: What's your suggestion?

G: How about going to visit the Three Gorges Museum? There, you can enjoy the beautiful pictures and videos of the Three Gorges, and get to know something about the history, folklore in this area, and the Dam Project.

T: That's a good idea.

G: I know that you are eager to see the lovely panda bears. I assure you that tomorrow will be a fine day, and we'll go to the zoo to see the panda bears. OK?

T: Perfect. Thank you.

Notes

① ... except that tourists from the countries that have signed visa-free agreements with China. ……来自与中国签署了免签协议国家的游客除外。

② equator province 靠近赤道的省份

③ ... or unexplained bleeding or bruising. ……或原因不明的出血或瘀伤。

Words and Expressions

notification	*n.* 通知;公告
submit	*v.* 提交,呈送
regretfully	*adv.* 抱歉地,遗憾地
deposit	*n.* 保证金,押金
Tibet	*n.* 西藏
Ebola	*n.* 埃博拉
equator	*n.* 赤道
hygiene	*n.* 卫生;保健
infected	*adj.* 感染的;受感染的
vomit	*v.* 呕吐
diarrhea	*n.* & *adj.* 腹泻;拉肚子
bleeding	*n.* & *v.* 出血;流血;失血 *adj.* 出血的
bruising	*v.* 擦伤,挫伤
symptom	*n.* 症状

visa-free	免签(证)
Congo	刚果
Guinea	几内亚
Liberia	利比里亚
Nigeria	尼日利亚
Sierra Leone	塞拉利昂
apply for	申请
go through	完成
be in order	就绪;妥当

panda bears	(口)大熊猫
weather forecast	天气预报
Three Gorges Museum	三峡博物馆
Dam Project	三峡大坝工程

Assignments

1. Write a letter according to the following conditions.

Receiver: Mr. & Mrs. Jones

Subject:通知对方长江三峡四日游已安排就绪,将于9月26日上午9点开始,9月26日早上8点在重庆机场集合后送上游船。附寄各种旅行文件。通知对方务必于9月22日前支付各项旅行费用。

2. Translate the following into English.

(1) 你们的中国10日游已经安排就绪。

(2) 我们将于2014年12月5日上午9点与你们在机场大厅会合。

(3) 请你务必于4月6日前支付你预订的香港7日游旅行费用,共1200美元。

(4) 如果你方付款在4月8日前未完成,我们将取消旅行安排。

(5) 我们建议旅游者近期避免前往日本旅行。

In-class Practice

Role-play

Find your partner and make a conversation about asking the guest to pay for the tour. Try to use the following patterns:

Your... trip to... is now in order.

Would you please make your payment by...?

How much is that?

How much should I pay?

Can I pay by credit card?

Broaden Your Mind

Travel Warning—Worldwide Caution

April 10, 2014

The Department of State has issued this Worldwide Caution to update information on the continuing threat of terrorist actions and violence against U. S. citizens and interests throughout the world. U. S. citizens are reminded to maintain a high level of vigilance and to take appropriate steps to increase their security awareness. This replaces the Worldwide Caution dated September 25, 2013, to provide updated information on security threats and terrorist activities worldwide.

The Department of State remains concerned about the continued threat of terrorist attacks, demonstrations, and other violent actions against U. S. citizens and interests overseas. Kidnapping and hostage events involving U. S. citizens have become increasingly prevalent as al Qa'ida and its affiliates(基地组织及其附属机构) have increased attempts to finance their operations through kidnapping for ransom operations. Al-Qa'ida in the Arabian Peninsula (AQAP) and al-Qa'ida in the Islamic Maghreb (AQIM)(伊斯兰马格里布) are particularly effective with kidnapping for ransom and are using ransom money to fund the range of their activities. Kidnapping targets are usually Western citizens from governments or third parties that have established a pattern of paying ransoms for the release of individuals in custody. Current information suggests that al-Qa'ida, its affiliated organizations, and other terrorist groups continue to plan and encourage kidnapping of U. S. citizens and Westerners. U. S. citizens should closely monitor Travel Warnings and Alerts, as well as Country Specific Information, on the Department of State's travel website to review the latest safety and security information for destination countries.

Situation on the Korean Peninsula

While the media continues to report on the heightened tensions on the Korean peninsula, they have also reported that the situation in South Korea is business as usual. Ministry of Foreign Affairs (MFA) has not issued any notice advising against travel to South Korea nor advised Singaporeans in South Korea to leave. Singaporeans residing in, or travelling to South Korea are encouraged to monitor the local developments through the media and their local contacts and to refer to the websites of MFA and the Singapore Embassy in Seoul for updates. Singaporeans are also urged to take all necessary precautions for their personal safety, including observing instructions by the local authorities. Singaporeans travelling overseas should Register with MFA at http://eregister.mfa.gov.sg/ and ensure that they have the appropriate insurance coverage. This will facilitate us to contact you.

Unit 17 Letters to Another Travel Service
给其他旅行社的信函

【内容导读】

本单元介绍旅行社间的往来业务信件，包括业务委托、报价、接待安排等的写作格式、写作要点及常用句型。

【学习目标】

掌握往来业务委托、报价、接待安排等信件写作格式、写作要点、常用句型与短语，并能熟练拟写。

【学习要点】

报价信函常用句型：

Would you please send us a copy of your catalogue and latest pricelist for. . . (tour) . . . ?

We have pleasure to offer you the following.

We are pleased to offer as follows.

We are sending herewith a copy of our latest price list for. . . .

Text

It is usual for a travel agency to have businesses with another travel service, like communication, cooperation, etc. one travel service may write to another travel service asking for an offer, receiving the tour group, or meeting the tourist.

Ⅰ. A Letter Asking for an Offer

Format and Main Contents

1. Asking for offer.

You may use:

We would appreciate it if you could supply more details and quotations for the following itineraries of. . . (tour). . . .

Would you please send us a copy of your catalogue and latest pricelist for. . . (tour). . . ?

Please let us have your latest prices for... (tour)....

2. Asking for reply/confirmation.

You may use:

We look forward to your early reply.

We look forward to receiving your confirmation at your earliest convenience.

Awaiting your reply at your earliest convenience.

Please confirm the booking as soon as payment is made by check.

Sample 1

Dear Mr. Zhang,
We would appreciate it if you could supply more details and quotations for the following itineraries of China Shandong Confucian Tour'99.
Tour 1, Confucian Home-town Study Tour①: Qingdao-Jinan-Tai'an-Qufu.
Tour 2, Following the Footsteps of Confucius②: Qufu-Zoucheng-Mount Tai-Zibo.
Awaiting your reply at your earliest convenience.
Yours truly,
John Masters

Sample 2

Dear Frederick,
We would appreciate it if you could supply more details and quotations for the following itinerary of six-day Adoption Tour Group Chongqing③ (15 persons):
Tour 1: Tour to the orphanage to receive babies (Chongqing-Fuling-Chongqing-Registration).
Tour 2: Half day tour to the zoo to see pandas.
Tour 3: Half day tour to the ancient town of Ciqikou.
Tour 4: Half day city tour.
Transfer to and from the airport and hotel.
Hotel: 7 double rooms and 1 single room at Hilton Hotel.
Guide: 1 English-speaking guide.
We look forward to your early reply.
Yours truly,
Lily

Ⅱ. A Letter for Making an Offer

Format and Main Contents

1. Thanks.
2. Making an offer (repeat and offer).

You may use:

We are pleased to offer as follows, subject to reply received here by... (date)....

In conformity/in accordance with the request in your letter of..., we have supplied quotations for the following itineraries.

We are sending herewith a copy of our latest price list for... for your reference.

In reply to your letter of..., we have pleasure to offer you the following.

Sample 1

Dear John Masters,

In conformity with the request in your letter of May 26, we have supplied quotations for the following itineraries:

Tour 1, Confucian Home-town Study Tour: Qingdao-Jinan-Tai'an-Qufu. RMB 3,500 per person.

Tour 2, Following the Footsteps of Confucius: Qufu-Zoucheng-Mount Tai-Zibo. RMB 3,200 per person.

We look forward to receiving your reservation.

Yours truly,

Zhang

Sample 2

Dear Deng,

In reply to your letter of Sept. 12, we are now making the following offer for the Canadian Adoption Group Chongqing (17 adults, 3 kids and 1 tour leader) from Nov. 26 to Nov. 30.

<table>
<tr><th colspan="2">Service Item</th><th>Rate RMB</th><th>Amount</th></tr>
<tr><td colspan="2">Tour coach
Air - conditioned tour coach for Transfers
to and from airport\hotel\registration center (twice)
City tour/sightseeing(3 times)</td><td>350 / one time</td><td>1,750RMB</td></tr>
<tr><td colspan="2">Luggage Van to and from airport (twice)</td><td>200 / one time</td><td>400RMB</td></tr>
<tr><td rowspan="2">Admission fee</td><td>The zoo (to see panda bears)</td><td>20 per person</td><td>400RMB</td></tr>
<tr><td>The Three Gorges Museum</td><td>40 per person</td><td>680RMB</td></tr>
<tr><td>Escort service charge</td><td>Translation and interpret for adoption process, sightseeing, and shopping</td><td>100 / day</td><td>500RMB</td></tr>
<tr><td>Total</td><td colspan="3">3,730RMB</td></tr>
<tr><td rowspan="3">Tips</td><td>1. For escort</td><td>150RMB/per family</td><td></td></tr>
<tr><td>2. For driver</td><td>50RMB/per family</td><td></td></tr>
<tr><td>3. For luggage boy</td><td>10RMB/per piece</td><td></td></tr>
<tr><td colspan="2">Remarks:</td><td colspan="2">1. No admission for the kids for the zoo.
2. Tips are paid by the guests.</td></tr>
</table>

Please confirm the above offer as soon as possible in order to make arrangements for this group.

Yours faithfully,

Frederick

Sample 3

Dear Lily,

In reply to your letter of Sept. 12, we have pleasure to offer you the following:

Total tour fares for a group of 15 persons: RMB 25,150

Including:

Bus fares for tour to the orphanage to receive babies (Chongqing-Fuling-Chongqing-Registration): RMB1,500

Bus fares and admission fees for half day tour to the zoo to see pandas: RMB800

Bus fares for half day tour to Ciqikou: RMB500

Bus fares and admission fees for half day city tour: RMB1,050

2 transfers to and from airport and hotel: RMB1,600

7 double rooms and 1 single room at Hilton Hotel: RMB19,200

Service fare for guide: RMB500

We look forward to your confirmation.

Yours truly,

Frederick

Oral Skills

Discussing Tour Arrangement

Procedure and Useful Patterns

Step 1 Start discussing tour arrangement.

Shall we start discussing the itinerary?

I drafted an itinerary for your tour. Would you go through it?

I'd like to know how you think about the tour plan.

It is well arranged. / Everything seems to be in order. But....

Step 2 Ask for an opinion or make a suggestion.

Have you got anything special in mind that you would like to visit?

Do you have some special demands about the tour?

What special requests do you have about the tour?

Is it possible for us to visit...?

Don't you think it would be better to visit...?

Why don't we spend more time in... instead of...?

Why not give up... and spend the time in...?

Most of the group members are fond of..., they might like to see (visit / enjoy)....

Sample Dialogue

(A = Local Guide; B = Tour Leader)

A: I'd like to know how you think about the tour plan I gave you yesterday.

B: Your itinerary is well arranged for regular tourists. But this time, since most of the members in this group are well educated people, they have some special demands about the tour.

A: What special requests do you have about the tour?

B: The group members are not at all satisfied with the tour arrangements. They have heard about the splendid constructions and palaces in Paris, but the Louvre Palace and the Notre Dame de Paris is not included in the itinerary.

A: You only stay in Paris for one day and a half. It is impossible for you to see all these places.

B: Why not give up the River Seine and spend the time in the Notre Dame?

A: That's a good idea.

B: And some of the group members are fond of French wines, if possible, they'd like to visit a vineyard and a wine brewery, and have a taste of the homemade wine from the cellar.

A: It's not a problem. On our way to Lyons, we'll stop at a vineyard with a brewery in it.[4]

B: Most of the group members have planned to buy French wines as gifts for their friends and relatives.

A: You are very thoughtful. I'll try my best to make your stay in France an enjoyable one.

B: You are so helpful. Thanks a lot.

Notes

① Confucian Home-town Study Tour 孔子故里修学游

② Following the Footsteps of Confucius 寻踪孔子游

③ Adoption Tour Group Chongqing 重庆团队收养游

④ On our way to Lyons, we'll stop at a vineyard with a brewery in it. 在去里昂的路途中,我们要在一个葡萄种植园停留,那里有个酿酒厂。

Words and Expressions

offer	*n.* 出价,开价
quotation	*n.* 报价;行市
catalogue	*n.* 产品目录
escort	*n.* 陪同
admission	*n.* 门票
vineyard	*n.* 葡萄种植园
brewery	*n.* 酿酒厂
cellar	*n.* 酒窖;地窖;储藏室
ask for an offer	要求对方报价
make an offer	向对方报价
Adoption Tour	收养旅游
Study Tour	修学旅游
luggage van	行李车
luggage boy	行李员
Louvre Palace	罗浮宫
Notre Dame de Paris	巴黎圣母院
Lyons	里昂(法国南部城市)

Assignments

1. Read carefully and translate the following letter into Chinese.

Dear gentlemen,

Would you please proceed with the ten-day China tour arrangement for the group, according to the itinerary enclosed and the following items:

(1) Members: 14 paying tourists and one free tour leader.

(2) Rooms required: 7 standard twin rooms and 1 single room.

(3) Hotels: White Swan Hotel—Guangzhou
Shanghai Hotel—Shanghai
Yanjing Hotel—Beijing.

(4) Transportation: By air-conditioned tour coach for all transfers and sightseeing.

(5) Meals: As prescribed in the itinerary.

(6) Guide: A German-speaking young guide.

We look forward to receiving your confirmation for the group at your earliest convenience.

Yours faithfully,

×××

2. Translate the following into English.

(1) 烦请寄给我一份你们的“长江三峡三日游”的最新价目表。

(2) 付款一经支付即请确认预订。

(3) 很高兴为你方询问的“中国十日游”作如下报价。

(4) 对于想参观的地方你有什么特别的想法吗?

(5) 如果有可能的话,我想去看看葡萄种植园并品尝一下地道的法国葡萄酒。

In-class Practice

Role-play

Divide the class into groups to discuss tour arrangement for one day city tour in Chongqing.

Broaden Your Mind

Climate Change: Appeal to Sustainable Tourism

The most recent IPCC(Intergovernmental Panel on Climate Change 政府间气候变化专门委员会) report on the effects of climate change (2013) shows it is being felt around the world. We need to both cut emissions and ensure that our infrastructure and ecosystems are prepared for a warmer world.

Few sectors encompass the range of challenges posed by climate change and water issues as fully as tourism. Tourists emit greenhouse gases as they fly across the globe. They stay in luxurious, water-intensive hotels. They consume food and other goods shipped in from around the world. Depending on what is included, tourism accounts for an estimated 4% to 10% of global emissions. Tourists demand infrastructure in locations, such as coastal resorts, that are particularly vulnerable to future climate change.

At the same time, tourists drive much positive change. The very fact that they value coastal areas, clean seas and beautiful scenery is what makes possible the protection of these resources in many places. Tourism generates 10% of global GDP; it is one of the fastest growing sectors and has a great multiplier effect. It provides valuable income to regions or even entire countries which might otherwise remain in poverty or see their young people migrate to cities. In some cases, tourism is a lever to protect a valuable habitat—a rainforest, a coral reef, a mangrove swamp—even in the face of other commercial pressures.

A less tangible, but perhaps even more important fact, is that tourism brings much of the world's populations into contact with new cultures, new peoples and new environments. These experiences teach us to value not only our own countries and communities, but also those around the world. These shared values are essential to confronting challenges such as climate change.

It is essential to reduce negative impacts while making the most of the benefits. Our countries have taken leading roles in this endeavour. For instance, airlines from Singapore and the UAE (United Arab Emirates 阿拉伯联合酋长国) are currently some of the most efficient in the world, with emissions per passenger kilometer being around 25% lower than the global average. Hotels can adopt cutting edge energy and water efficiency measures. Tourism can also be made more sustainable by means of broader measures, such as the increased use of renewable energy in all countries. The UAE has made a Green Growth Strategy, including tourism, the core of its development strategy. Some countries, such as Costa Rica, have made "eco-tourism" their main strategy for attracting tourists.

The international community has also recognized the importance of making tourism more sustainable in many venues. The World Tourism Organization not only stresses the three pillars of sustainable development—economic, social, and environmental—but also accords a specific section to the unique challenge of climate change. Certain progress has been made in fighting climate change as part of the UNFCCC negotiations, but we still have far to go. The World Economic Forum in Davos in January 2014 will again look at climate change and the economic dimensions of addressing it. In September 2014, U. N. Secretary-General Ban Ki-moon will invite world leaders to participate in the Climate Summit. Their shared goal will be to mobilise action and ambition regarding climate change to keep the rise in average global temperatures at 2 degrees Celsius above pre-industrial levels. This will provide another opportunity for us to reconcile the need for economic development and climate protection. Tourism is showing us both the challenges and opportunities of this effort.

Although we may have different ideas, economies, policies, and philosophies, we live with the environment and will continue to depend on it.

Unit 18 Itinerary and Tour Conditions
游程与旅游合同

【内容导读】

本单元介绍游程安排的基本原则，英语游程安排表的内容、格式和表述方法。介绍英语旅游合同的基本项目、内容、排列格式及常用术语。

【学习目标】

掌握并能设计、制作英语游程安排表。

【学习要点】

游程安排(Itinerary)

词汇与短语：visit to. . . , guided walk, transfer, bus tour, typical, hiking, cruise

Text

Making an Itinerary

An itinerary is a tour schedule. It is the plan and arrangement for a tour at a place. While the itinerary schemed by the local guide is more detailed, it is usually exact to indicate the activity on the tour basis. ① An itinerary is made before the arrival of a tour group. It is made according to the reception program.

Basically, the itinerary should be detailed enough to cover not only the food, lodging, transport, and travel of the tourists, but also the shopping, entertainment and some other related activities. For making an itinerary, the feature of tourist attractions, tourists' requests (both the visitors' physical and spiritual wellbeing②), tour season, tour time, and even climate or weather should be taken into consideration. And the schedule planning should observe the following principles:

- The schedule should not be too crowded.
- Don't copy an old schedule all the time.
- Don't forget to set free time for the tourists.

The tour schedule is divided into two types: daily schedule and one-day schedule. Generally, the following six parts should be included for a tour schedule:

① tour date / time;

② travel route;

③ destination and features of attractions;

④ arrangements for meals and accommodations;

⑤ transportation means;

⑥ activities.

Sample Itinerary 1

Happiness Tour Group

Day 1 14:30 Arrival at Beijing Airport
15:10 Transfer to Yanjing Hotel
20:00 Bus tour-Beijing by night

Day 2 9:00 Visit to Tian'Anmen Square
10:00 Guided walk through the Forbidden City (Imperial Palace)
13:00 Roast Beijing Duck at Quanjude
15:00 Stop at Qianmen for shopping
20:00 Evening at Beijing Opera House

Day 3 7:00 Day trip to the Great Wall and the Ming Tombs. Evening free

Day 4 8:00 Visit to the Temple of Heaven
12:00 Lunch at the Summer Palace
13:00 Boating on the Kunming Lake
16:00 Guided walk through Beijing University
20:00 Evening at a typical Beijing Teahouse

Day 5 9:00 Departure from hotel for airport

Sample Itinerary 2

Daily Schedule for U.S. Adoption Group

Subject to arrival times, actual document processing timeline, and orphanage procedure, etc. your flexibility is appreciated.

Day 1 Group arrives in Chongqing. Check in to Holiday Inn Yangtze. Fill out the adoption application forms in the hotel meeting room.

Day 2 At 7:30a. m. go to the Fuling Orphanage (two-hour ride by bus) to receive the baby.

At 11:00a. m. come back to the hotel.

At 2:30p. m. go to the registration office to complete paperwork.

Day 3 Half day tour to the zoo to see panda bears in the morning. Afternoon and evening free.

Day 4 Half day tour to Chaotianmen, the People's Great Hall and the Three Gorges Museum in the morning. Afternoon and evening free.

Day 5 Optional half day tour to Eling Park to have a bird's eye view of Chongqing. Pay as you go. ③ Receive and check notary paper in the afternoon.

Day 6 Receive babies' passports. Pack luggage. Leave Chongqing for Guangzhou on Flight 3U345 at 19:35p. m. / 21:20p. m.

Tour Conditions

Tour condition, also called Tour Contract, is an agreement signed between the tourists and the travel service. And it will go into effect, since it is signed by both parties.

The tour condition usually includes:

Service start & Service end

Members

Service items

Including accommodations, meals, transportation and guide

Other items

Indicate service fare not included or to be excluded

Sample

Package Tour Conditions for Travel in China

Date: April 15, 2005

Ref:

Service start: April 20, 2005

Service end: April 30, 2005

Members: Fourteen paying tourists, one free tour leader

Service Items:

accommodations: 7 double rooms for tourists and 1 single room for the conductor, each with a shower at 3-star hotels including service charge and taxes.

meals: meals throughout, including meals at restaurants of local flavor.

transfer: by air-conditioned motorcar to and from airports, railway stations, hotels, restaurants, wharf and wherever required.

transportation: soft berth railway transportation, economy class airplane transportation and standard cabins on deluxe cruiser for traveling on the Yangtze River.

sightseeing: by motorcar, including admission fee.

guide: English-speaking guide for all sightseeing and shopping.

gratuities: to hotel boys, restaurant waiters.

Service fare not included:

(1) Airport taxes;

(2) Drinks, wine, laundry for individual purposes;

(3) All other expenses of a personal nature.

Party A	Party B
(signature)	(signature)

Oral Skills

Talking about Itinerary

Procedure and Useful Patterns

Step 1 Draw the guests' attention.

Ladies and gentlemen, now I'm talking about the itinerary for your trip.

I hope you can spare me some time to talk about the itinerary for your trip.

Step 2 Introduce the tour arrangement (go over the schedule).

We have arranged... for you.

First, you will sightsee in....

Then, you will go to....

After... you'll go to visit....

Step 3 Seek the views of the guests.

Do you have any special suggestions?

What do you say to this itinerary?

Sample Dialogue

Guide: Good evening, ladies and gentlemen. I hope you can spare me some time to talk about the itinerary for your trip. ④

Guest: Fine.

Guide: Well, you had received a copy of the itinerary from our travel service before you came, right?

Guest: Yes, we did. Are there any changes?

Guide: No, not at all. We'll just go over it again. Well, first you will sightsee in Beijing for 4 days. Then you will go to Chengde Mountain Resort. From there you will move to visit Qufu.

Guest: That's the hometown of Confucius, right?

Guide: That's right. After that you go to Suzhou by train and spend two days there before going to Shanghai. After spending another two days in Shanghai, you'll go to visit beautiful Hangzhou. From there, you'll fly to Guilin.

Guest: And we leave China from Guangzhou?

Guide: Correct. You'll fly directly to Guangzhou from Guilin. And then you leave for Hong Kong by boat.

Guest: Great.

Guide: The whole trip will be lasting 16 days. I hope that everybody in this group be physically fit for this long trip.

Guest: No problem. Everybody is as strong as a horse. ⑤

Guide: Good. Do you have any questions?

Guest: When do we get a chance to see the giant pandas? You know everybody is eager to see them.

Guide: You'll see them tomorrow morning when we visit the zoo.

Guest: Perfect! Thank you very much for everything you've done for us.

Guide: My pleasure.

Notes

① While the itinerary schemed by the local guide is more detailed, it is usually exact to indicate the activity on the tour basis. 尽管地陪设计的游程更为详细，通常也需要准确地标明旅游基本活动。

② both the visitors' physical and spiritual wellbeing 游客的生理和精神愉悦

③ Pay as you go. 如参加需付费。

④ I hope you can spare me some time to talk about the itinerary for your trip. 我希望你们给我点时间谈谈你们的旅行行程安排。

⑤ Everybody is as strong as a horse. 每个人都健壮如牛。

Words and Expressions

combination	*n.* 组合；结合
flexibility	*n.* 灵活；灵活性
optional	*adj.* 可选择的
notary	*n.* 公证；公证人
wharf	*n.* 码头
cabin	*n.* （船）客舱
cruiser	*n.* 游船；游轮
gratuity	*n.* 小费
sightsee	*v.* 观光
physically	*adv.* 身体上；体格上
Confucius	孔子
leave for	出发去（某地）
subject to	受到；由于

Assignments

1. Make an itinerary for the guests according to the following situations.

One-day city tour in Chongqing for a group of 20 college students from Korea.

2. Translate the following into English.

(1) 明天我们将前往世界文化遗产地大足石刻参观。

(2) 晚上 6 点,小天鹅餐馆晚餐,重庆火锅。

(3) 住宿要求:8 间标准间、2 间大床房,五星级酒店。

(4) 在上海期间,我们所有的参观游览、购物需要一位英语导游。

(5) 他健壮如牛,能适应这次长途旅行。

In-class Practice

Role-play

Divide the class into groups (travel service clerk, guests) to discuss package tour conditions for a 10-day trip to Thailand.

Broaden Your Mind

Karst Landforms in Wulong

Wulong Karst, an important part of South China Karst, is situated at the lower reaches of the Wujiang River southeast of Chongqing. It was named as a world natural heritage by UNESCO in 2007. Wulong Karst features spectacular karst landscapes, including the three main parts of Lotus Cave, Three Natural Bridges and Houping Giant Doline (Houping Tiankeng).

Wulong Karst is a valuable treasure that nature created. It is a cluster of several karst landscapes, consisting of gorges, natural bridges, caves, eroded doline, shafts and underground streams. These karst landforms developed in the carbonate rocks, vividly recording the development and evolution of karst terrain in the Three Gorges area since Pleistocene Era.

Three Natural Bridges is located 20 kilometers (12 miles) southeast of Chongqing City in Wulong County. It is a rare geological wonder and an eco-tourist's delight. It features three natural karst bridges: Tianlong Bridge, Qinglong Bridge and Heilong Bridge. The three natural karst stone arch bridges, with an average height of over 200 meters (656 feet), and an average span of over 200 meters (656 feet), constitute the largest natural bridge cluster in Asia.

The three natural bridges are situated in a 1.5 kilometers (12 miles) —long gorge. They evolved due to tectonic uplift and the erosion by underground water. Some parts uplifted forming the bridges, and others collapsed to form karst pits. Therefore, the unique landscape of "Three Natural Bridges enclosed with Two Pits" is solely nature's creation.

Tianlong Bridge is about 200 meters (656 feet) in height, 100 meters (328 feet) in width. It spans 450 meters (1,476 feet), and has two arches from south to north. The south arch was also called Mihun Cave. The northern arch is a passage. Qinglong Bridge is about 350 meters (1,148 feet) high, 150 meters (492 feet) wide, and spans over 400 meters (1,312 feet). After the rains, a waterfall pours over the bridge and forms a mist. When the sunset reflects on the mist, a colorful rainbow emerges like a dragon ascending to the heaven. Heilong Bridge has a deep and long arch passage, like a black dragon winding its way out from the passage. Heilong Bridge is also renowned for its four springs with tortuous trickles of stream. The Three Natural Bridges is a karst stone arch bridge cluster unrivalled elsewhere of Asia in terms of height and the thickness of the bridge surface. It is magnificent.

Unit 19 Dealing with Complaints
投诉处理

【内容导读】

本单元通过实例介绍旅游投诉信件及回复信函的英文写作格式、内容与常用表达方式。同时,本单元还介绍旅游投诉处理的英语口语技能。

【学习目标】

通过本单元的学习,掌握旅游投诉回复信件的英文写作格式、内容与常用表达方式;掌握面对游客投诉的处理原则、程序、方法等英语口语技能。

【学习要点】

投诉处理常用句型:

I feel terribly sorry to hear what you said. Something must be done about it.

We hope that you could accept our sincere apology for the mess we made.

I do apologize for the inconvenience.

As a gesture of our goodwill I am sending a refund of. . . .

We shall mail you a check of. . . in compensation for. . . .

Text

Tourism industries will have to deal with so many tourists with different needs and wants, and opinions. Occasional errors are a natural part of doing business even under the best conditions. Never view the tourists' complaints as an unwelcome surprise. ① It is far better for tourism industries to receive too many complaints than none at all. This is because that the tourist's complaints may highlight the inefficiency in our management or services. Each complaint is an opportunity to better our work. Therefore, we must be ready all the time to settle the tourists' complaints. By effectively solving and handling a complaint, we will be able to improve our operation and may transform an angry customer into a lasting friend who will recommend our service to other customers. ②

Ⅰ. A Letter for Complaint

Format and Main Contents

Useful patterns:

In writing such a letter, it is better to make the letter brief and to the point. Try to avoid writing an angry, sarcastic, or threatening letter. The person reading your letter probably was not responsible for your problem but may be very helpful in resolving it.

1. State all important facts about the trip.

(including the date, place, and any information about the problems during the trip)

You may use:

I' m writing to complain about....

I am disappointed with your service because....

The service was inadequate / not performed correctly.

I was billed the wrong amount.

I regret to inform you that the product is defective and my numerous verbal complaints to your personnel have yielded no results.

2. State what you want done about the problem.

You may use:

Please give (half / 30% of) my money back, or I shall be forced to take the matter further.

To resolve the problem, I would appreciate it if you could....

I request you to either replace the product with a functioning new product or refund my money within one week.

I look forward to your immediate action on this occasion.

I look forward to hearing from you and to a resolution of this problem.

3. Enclosure: all document copies regarding your problem.

You may use:

Enclosed is a copy / are copies of the receipt / contract etc.

I am enclosing a copy of the receipt, to help you initiate immediate action.

Sample 1

To Whom It May Concern:

I am writing regarding a tour that my wife and I took with your company on June 26, 2012. The itinerary stated that we would see some of the most interesting sights of the city. Since we had visited the city before, we looked forward to seeing some new attractions.

On the morning of June 26, our tour guide picked us up in a small van. It did not look like any tour bus I had ever seen. He drove us to the waterfront area and said that we could explore the area on our own. The tour guide said that he had to leave for a short time to arrange for our lunch. By the time the tour guide came back, three hours had gone by! I was very angry and confronted him. I told him that this was the worst tour I had ever been on.

I am asking for a complete refund of the price of the tour. Please send a check to the address above for $ 150 at your earliest convenience.

Enclosed is a copy of the receipt for the tour.

Sincerely,

×××

Sample 2

Dear Sir:

I'm writing to complain about the two-day trip to China mainland from Hong Kong organized by your travel agency. It was stated in the tour contract that a professional tour guide would lead 20 tourists as a team, but actually, the tour guide even did not know the exact tour route and there were 30 people in our team. Besides, it was claimed that we would visit five tourist destinations, while in fact we only visited three places of interest. Worse still, we not only had to pay for our meals except lunch, but also four people were arranged to share one room in a poorly-equipped hotel in Shenzhen, which was totally different from the tour contract that two tourists share a room in a four-star hotel and meals were included in the package.

I am enclosing copies of the receipt and the contract. Please give half of my money back, or I shall be forced to take the matter further.

Thank you for your consideration.

Yours sincerely,

×××

Ⅱ. A Reply Letter

It is important to deal quickly with letters of complaint. A prompt and satisfactory reply may save a customer. Make sure whether the complaint is justified. If you are sure the customer is at fault, your reply should politely point out what the facts are. If there is any doubt about responsibility for a mistake, it is often wiser to take it as true that the customer is right.

Format and Main Contents

1. Express your thanks.

Useful patterns:

Thank you for your letter of... concerning....

2. Apologize for the mistake, and explain why it happened.

Useful patterns:

I feel terribly sorry to hear what you said. Something must be done about it.

Please forgive what we did to you and accept our sincere apology.

We hope that you could accept our sincere apology for the mess we made.

I do apologize for the inconvenience.

3. Explain what action you are taking.

Useful patterns:

As a gesture of our goodwill I am sending a refund of....

We shall mail you a check of... in compensation for....

We would have refund and hope that you could accept our sincere apology for the mess we made.

We do wish you could be satisfied with what we have compensated for the trouble we made.

Sample

Dear Mr. Allen,

Thank you for your letter of June 30 concerning your two-day trip to China mainland.

We have checked with the tour arrangement, the tour guide and the bus driver, it is clear that it is our responsibility for the mistake. We do apologize for your inconvenience.

As a gesture of our goodwill we are sending a refund of $ 100. ③ We do wish you could be satisfied with what we have compensated for the trouble we made.

Yours sincerely,

× × ×

Oral Skills

Dealing with Complaints

Procedures and Useful Patterns

Step 1 Listen to the tourist attentively.

Useful patterns:

Anything I can do for you, sir?

What's happened?

Can you be more specific about what is wrong with... ?

Step 2 Say "sorry" and give necessary explanation.

Useful patterns:

I'm awfully sorry to hear that. You see, it is the busy season for travel.

We are terribly sorry for all this mess. You see, it has just opened, and it is rather short-staffed.

We do apologize for the inconvenience. We are terribly understaffed.

Step 3 Take actions to solve the problem.

Useful patterns:

Well, I'll tell the manager right now to see if we can... for you.

We'll do... at once.

We are working to correct this mistake immediately.

Step 4 Check back with the tourist.

Sample Dialogue 1

(G = Guest, T = Tour Guide)

T: Anything I can do for you, sir?

G: Of course, you can do a lot for me.

T: What's happened?

G: You see, the room you arranged for me is near a noisy place, and the air-conditioner doesn't work well. It's too warm here, and I can't sleep.

T: I'm awfully sorry to hear that. Have you tried turning the switch to "L" position?

G: Of course, but it is of no use.

T: I'm sorry. You know, it is the busy season for travel. And many hotels are full.

G: I don't care that. I'm unsatisfied with my room, and I need a quiet and cool room.

T: Well, I'll tell the manager right now to see if we can find another room for you. Just a moment please.

T: (A moment later) Sir, we've got a vacant room, Rm. 1215. It's higher up and at the back of the hotel. If you please get your luggage ready, the bell boy will collect them and show you where it is.

G: That's very kind of you. Thank you.

T: You are welcome. Good night. Have a good sleep.

Sample Dialogue 2

(G = Guest; W = Mr. Wang, the tour guide)

G: Mr. Wang, I have a problem with the meal.

W: What's wrong, Madam?

G: We only have hot tea to drink, four cold dishes for the ten people at our table, and some of the food is too strange to eat.

W: So, you mean you don't have enough food to eat, or appropriate drinks, and you don't like the food, right?

G: Yes, I'm very upset. We've been sightseeing all morning and everybody is quite hungry.

W: Well, Madam. Today's lunch is a Chinese banquet. It is our tradition that a few cold dishes are brought out first and as these are finished the next dishes are served. By this way we can enjoy each dish while it is hot and fresh.

G: Oh, I see. But this does not solve the other problems.

W: The restaurant also serves soft drinks if you do not like tea.

G: That will help some, but what about the food?

W: Can you be more specific about what is wrong with the food?④

G: Yes. It is strange looking. I've eaten Chinese food at home and it never looks like this. I cannot tell what some of the food is. I've never seen these things before.

W: I understand, Madam. This is not what you thought to be Chinese food, but have you tasted it?

G: No, I'll not try anything strange to me.

W: Well, I'll tell the waitress to introduce the dishes slowly and clearly. And let me suggest that you just try to taste it, Madam. I think you will find it quite delicious or at least better than you thought. There are also more to come so I think you will find enough to your liking.

G: Will there be some meat?

W: Yes, we'll be eating fish, pork and chicken.

G: Good, because I need more than just vegetables.

W: Well, Madam. I've never heard of anyone starving while visiting China, so try parts of the meal and when it is over we can talk again to avoid any future problems.

G: OK, that sounds like a good idea.

Notes

① Never view the tourists' complaints as an unwelcome surprise. 千万不要把游客的抱怨视为不受欢迎的诧异之事。

② ... and may transform an angry customer into a lasting friend who will good-mouth our service. ……或许可以把一位生气的顾客转变为持久的朋友,他(她)将为我们的服务带来良好的口碑。

③ As a gesture of our goodwill we are sending a refund of \$ 100. 我们寄上 100

美元退款,以作为我们善意的表示。

④ Can you be more specific about what is wrong with the food? 关于食物的问题你能说得更具体一点吗?

Words and Expressions

complaint	*n.* 投诉;抱怨
complain	*v.* 投诉;抱怨
highlight	*v.* 使突出;把…照亮
inefficiency	*n.* 不足
sarcastic	*adj.* 讥讽的,嘲讽的
refund	*v.* 退款
initiate	*v.* 启动;开始,发起
waterfront	*n.* 海滨;江边
confront	*v.* 面对;使面对面
short-staffed	*adj.* 人手短缺的,人手不足的
understaffed	*adj.* 人员不足的,人手不够的
specific	*adj.* 明确的;具体的
appropriate	*adj.* 适当的;合适的
transform... into...	使…转变成…

Assignments

1. Read the following letter of complaint carefully and write a letter of reply which includes:

(1) Express your pity on hearing the complaint;

(2) State the ways to cope with the problem;

(3) Apologize for the trouble you brought.

Dear Sir or Madam: I'm writing to you to complain about my holiday your travel agency arranged for me. When my wife and I arrived at the hotel, we found it was near a busy market and as a result we found it was hard for the whole week. The food was terrible and the price was too high. The assistants were rude and often not able to understand us. In addition to this, we were most unhappy with the arrangement for the day trips that were part of our holiday package. The buses were always crowded, and arrived late. One of them even did not arrive at all. We had expected a pleasant holiday, and we were very disappointed. I look forward to hearing from you and to a resolution of this problem. Sincerely yours, ×××

2. Translate the following into English.

(1) 客人要求全额退还旅行费用。

(2) 为了表示我们的歉意,我们将寄给你200美元的退款。

(3) 给你造成了不便,请接受我们真诚的道歉。

(4) 关于旅游车的问题能否请您说得更详细一点?

(5) 我希望你们给出一个解决问题的方案。

In-class Practice

Role-play

A tourist is trying to refund a Chinese paper fan he bought yesterday, because the fan becomes loose, but the shop assistant insists exchanging another one for him. Find your partner and make a conversation. Try to use the following patterns:

Can you tell me why you want to refund it?

Are you sure you bought it in our shop?

I still kept the receipt.

We can't refund it, but we can exchange another one for you.

Broaden Your Mind

Harmonious Society

Since China introduced its reform and opening-up policies in 1978, profound changes have taken place in the economy and in the domestic and international environments. It is against such a backdrop that the Chinese Government has raised the goal of building a harmonious society.

Currently, China's economy is a socialist market economy. But some drawbacks of the planned economy still remain and the market economy is neither mature nor complete. Our society has many contradictions and uncertain factors in it, such as huge gaps in income, increasingly serious problems facing rural areas, farmers and agriculture, the drainage of farmland, heavy pressure in the workplace and an incomplete social security system.

But, more than two decades of reform and opening-up have brought about tangible achievements in China's economic development. People's living standards have been greatly improved and the number of poor people has decreased by a large number. Job opportunities have increased and deep-seated problems are being solved step by step. A harmonious society featuring orderly competition and honesty is taking shape.

What are the main characteristics of a harmonious society? It will put people first and make all social activities beneficial to people's subsistence, enjoyment and development. In a harmonious society, the political environment is stable, the economy is prosperous, people live in peace and work in comfort and social welfare improves.

These goals should be demonstrated in the following areas:

As the economy grows, people's living standards should increase gradually. As the essence of a harmonious society is affluence, the development of a country should go from being moderately well-off into being well-off and affluent; from having big gaps in income to narrowing gaps; from dealing with poverty to eliminating poverty.

In a harmonious society people at all levels respect each other. Labour, knowledge, technology and capital are all factors of wealth creation, which can make profits and should be respected so long as they have made contributions to society. A harmonious society should see honest, friendly and harmonious relationships and just, fair and open competition between social members, regions and departments. In such a society, competition will optimize the distribution of resources, foster technological progress, develop social productivity and raise overall national strength.

A harmonious society advocates an overall, co-ordinated and sustainable development concept, making the interests of different sectors balanced. A harmonious society should also see great improvements in morals and education. The strategy of invigorating the nation by education should be followed and elementary education and higher education universalized. Various academic theories should flourish. China has attached much importance to education, particularly compulsory education. The central government has planned fee exemptions and subsidies for students in 592 poor counties included in the national poverty-relief programme by 2007. Some experts want to extend the policy to poor families both in urban and rural areas.

In addition, a harmonious society is also manifested by the gradual improvement of the legal system and standardized social management. A harmonious society is a society with the rule of law, where there is ordered market competition, strict market management and standard market behaviour.

All people should co-exist harmoniously, love and help each other, encourage each other and make an effort to contribute to the building of a harmonious society.

参 考 文 献

[1]王宁.饭店与旅游英语.成都:四川科学技术出版社,2001.

[2]王琳,关铁山.旅游英语应用教程.北京:高等教育出版社,2011.

[3]魏国富.实用旅游英语教程.上海:复旦大学出版社,2002.

[4]朱岐新,张秀桂.英语导游翻译必读.北京:中国旅游出版社,1999.

[5]周玮.旅行社英语.广州:广东旅游出版社,1999.

[6]陈克成等.旅游交际英语通.上海:华东师范大学出版社,1992.

[7]刘玉玲,李四新.旅游英语.武汉:武汉测绘科技大学出版社,1998.

[8]高晓芳,张琴.外事英语.武汉:武汉测绘科技大学出版社,1997.

[9]郗庆华.导游英语会话.天津:南开大学出版社,1999.

[10]杨天庆.四川英语导游应试必备手册.成都:四川科学技术出版社,2002.

[11]姚宝荣,陈慧,黄建敏.模拟导游实务英语教程.北京:高等教育出版社,2008.

[12]袁智敏.领队英语.北京:旅游教育出版社,2013.

[13]王宁.旅游翻译质量与旅游地形象——旅游翻译中的问题评析.重庆工商大学学报,2005,22(1):137-140.